Nelson Mandela
A Legendary Story

By
Mamta Sharma Ghuge

NELSON MANDELA – A LEGENDARY STORY

First Edition: 2012
4th Impression: 2014

All rights reserved. No part of this book may be reproduced, stored in a retrieval system or transmitted, in any form or by any means, mechanical, photocopying, recording or otherwise, without any prior written permission of the publisher.

© with the publisher

Published by Kuldeep Jain for

An imprint of
B. JAIN PUBLISHERS (P) LTD.
1921/10, Chuna Mandi, Paharganj, New Delhi 110 055 (INDIA)
Tel.: +91-11-4567 1000 • *Fax:* +91-11-4567 1010
Email: info@bjain.com • *Website:* **www.bjain.com**

Printed in India by
J.J. Offset Printers

ISBN: 978-81-319-1132-7

Dedication

Dedicated to all
those who believe in fighting for a cause

Acknowledgements

I would like to thank my children Ambika, Anant and Aishwarya, the little one, for being so patient with me. Special thanks to my long time friend Udita for doing so much for me. Gratitude is also extended to all the friends and well wishers who have been with me in the struggle called life.

Publisher's Note

One of the best ways to understand the complex human nature and the world is through reading biographies. Biographies of different personalities can help us understand what are the different aspects of things which make or break a person. What are the issues which cause war and what are the aspects which bring peace in human life. What is something a person earns for and what is something which can make a person change his entire perspective. What are those life turning incidences which affect human mind and psychology. The lives of the successful can teach you how to go about enriching your life and creating your own future. You can learn from their mistakes and victories.

People are always interested to read about people who inspire them. But there are many facts which remain hidden from the general public. The idea of bringing this series of biographies is to bring out those facts which have till date not been made public or made available at one platform. The author Mamta Sharma Ghuge has done extensive research to explore the inside out of the person's life who is being written about and has brought out many facts which remained hidden before.

We hope you like this series of books and would be happy to get a feedback from you.

Kuldeep Jain

C.E.O., B. Jain Publishers (P) Ltd.

Contents

Dedication iii
Acknowledgements v
Publisher's Note vii

CHAPTERS

Chapter 1   Introduction 1
Chapter 2   Fact File 5
Chapter 3   Childhood and Early Years 11
Chapter 4   Marriage and Family 15
Chapter 5   Apartheid 19
Chapter 6   African National Congress 31
Chapter 7   The Sharpeville and Boipatong Massacres 37
Chapter 8   Wind of Change 43
Chapter 9   The Arms Deal Saga 47
Chapter 10   Nelson Mandela and Gandhi 53
Chapter 11   The Shifting Sands of Illusion 59
Chapter 12   The Trials 67

Chapter 13 The Prison Years 79
Chapter 14 The Victory 89
Chapter 15 Negotiating Peace 95
Chapter 16 The Leader 99
Chapter 17 Deepest Fear 103
Chapter 18 The Controversies 105
Chapter 19 The Nobel Peace Prize 115
Chapter 20 Accolades and Honors 121
Chapter 21 International Affairs 127
Chapter 22 Nelson Mandela and the Media 135
Chapter 23 Beyond Politics 145
Chapter 24 A Living Legend 157
Bibliography 165

Chapter 1
Introduction

It was 4.14 pm, on the afternoon of 11 February, 1990 when Nelson Mandela, the world's best known political prisoner walked away from the Victor Verster detention centre, outside Cape Town, South Africa. He was free at last after twenty seven years in captivity. It was indeed a great emotional moment of contemporary history. Nelson Mandela had been imprisoned for masterminding the armed struggle of the African National Congress (ANC) to overthrow the apartheid regime in South Africa. Today, he is not just an African legend but an international icon symbolizing one of the greatest struggles against atrocities committed by the human species against its own kind.

Being set free was not the end but the beginning of a long drawn fight for Nelson Mandela and his supporters. Mandela said, "These countless human beings, both inside and outside our country, had the nobility of spirit to stand in the path of tyranny and injustice, without seeking selfish gain. They recognized that an injury to one is an injury to all and therefore acted together in defense of justice and a common human decency." He had already been branded as a terrorist, but his resolve to see South Africa free and on the path of democracy grew stronger by the day. The sensitive issue was not just leading his people to victory but seeing to it that the country does not get engulfed into a civil war and ensuring peaceful transition.

Nelson Mandela refused to compromise with the evil he saw even at the cost of his own personal freedom. Facing a stiff prison term for his anti-government activities, in 1964, Mandela made the following statement before the court:

"During my lifetime I have dedicated myself to this struggle of the African people. I have fought against white domination and I have fought against black domination. I have cherished the ideal of a democratic and free society in which all persons live together in harmony and with equal opportunities. It is an ideal which I hope to live for and to achieve. But if need be, it is an ideal for which I am prepared to die."

The refusal to ever give in, astonishing understanding and forgiveness for those who disagreed—this is Nelson Mandela, a trustworthy politician and an international statesman with incomparable moral influence. He had grown up in a country where people could be jailed for drinking from a wrong water fountain, get less pay for the same job because of their skin color, where they were repeatedly told by the government that they were savages. Growing up in South Africa meant that all these things and even worse became an integral part of the daily lives. Instead of reconciling with this reality, Nelson Mandela decided to start a long and arduous journey that would eventually culminate into ending apartheid. Apartheid will be forgotten but Nelson Mandela will be remembered as a true freedom fighter.

"I have walked that long road to freedom. I have tried not to falter; I have made missteps along the way. But I have discovered the secret that after climbing a great hill, one only finds that there are many more hills to climb. I have taken a moment here to rest, to steal a view of the glorious vista that surrounds me, to look back on the distance I have come. But I can rest only for a moment, for with freedom comes responsibilities, and I dare not linger, for my long walk is not yet ended."—Nelson Mandela

On 10 May, 1994, Nelson Mandela took over as the first democratically elected President of South Africa and continued until June 1999. This marked the transition from the white minority rule. The challenges were in plenty—improvement of the lives of indigenous population and controlling the HIV epidemic continued to be of serious concern. These were the real enemies that had to be overcome. Towards the whites, free South Africa followed a policy of reconciliation and managed to win their trust. "No one is born hating another person because of the color of his skin, or his background, or his religion. People must learn to hate, and if they can learn to hate, they can be taught to love, for love comes more naturally to the human heart than its opposite." This approach was unique in nature and was acclaimed worldwide. Nelson Mandela continues to actively participate in educational programs and undertake initiatives like 'Make Poverty History Campaign'.

Mandela's name echoes with the struggle for independence and social, political and institutional rights of the people of South Africa. "A good head and a good heart are always a formidable combination...I learned that courage was not the absence of fear, but the triumph over it. The brave man is not he who does not feel afraid, but he who conquers that fear." Fearless and determined to reach the destination, Nelson Mandela made history by becoming a universal symbol of social justice. For years he lived in jails, cut off from the mainstream society and was the longest detained political prisoner. Nelson Mandela is one of the very few African leaders who relinquished power voluntarily. After stepping down from the Presidency, he helped establish the Nelson Mandela Foundation, an organization committed to social justice and reconciliation.

This biography is a humble attempt to take the readers on a fascinating voyage of getting to know the life of a great man – his ambitions and his aspirations. The various roles that he fulfilled in his life successfully not only made him an icon but one of the most inspirational leaders of the twentieth century. To the teeming millions around the world Nelson Mandela stands, like no other living figure does, for the triumph of dignity and hope over despair and hatred, of self-discipline and love over persecution and evil.

Chapter 2
Fact File

- Born on 18 July, 1918 in the little village of Mvezo, in Qunu in southern Transkei, into the royal family of the Tembu, a Xhosa-speaking tribe.
- 1941—Mandela meets Walter Sisulu, an active member of the ANC who supported him with work and finances. Both become good friends.
- 1944—Mandela joins the ANC and helps establishing of the ANC Youth League. He married his first wife, Evelyn Mase the same year.
- 1947—Mandela is elected secretary of the ANC Youth League.
- 1949—The Youth League's 'Program of Action' to achieve full citizens and direct parliamentary representation for all South Africans is adopted by the ANC at its annual conference advocating the use of boycotts, strikes, civil disobedience and non-cooperation.
- 1950-51—Mandela is elected to the ANC National Executive Committee and as the national president of the Youth League in 1951.

- 1953—ANC banned; Mandela resigns officially and is forced to go underground.

- 1956—Mandela, Tambo, Sisulu and 153 others are arrested for high treason and charges under the Suppression of Communism Act.

- 1957—Mandela meets Winnie and marries her after divorcing his first wife.

- 1959—ANC splits and Pan-Africanist Congress (PAC) is formed which is the radical wing of ANC, advocating direct action against the apartheid regime.

- 1962—Mandela leaves South Africa illegally to attend a freedom conference in Algeria for fund raising from African states and resolves to extend it to Western and socialist nations. He is arrested on return and jailed for five years.

- 1973—Apartheid is declared as 'a crime against humanity' by the United Nations.

- 1975—Portuguese withdraw from Angola and Mozambique paving the path for installation of new independent governments antagonistic towards the apartheid regime in South Africa. The ANC sets up military bases in Angola.

- 1982—Mandela and Sisulu are transferred from Robbin Island to the high security Pollsmoor Prison on mainland.

- 1983—The United Democratic Front (UDF), a coalition of around 600 organizations is formed to negotiate the end of apartheid. Bishop Desmond Tutu emerges as one of the principal spokesmen.

- 1988—Mandela is diagnosed with tuberculosis and is moved to the Victor Verster Prison near Paarl near Cape Town. South African President, Botha directs his chief of intelligence to secretly meet Mandela to explore the possibilities of a peace settlement.
- 1989—Mandela and Botha meet face to face at the Presidential office. Mandela refuses to give any undertaking. Botha resigns following a stroke and F W de Klerk, a moderate takes over. Negotiations for Mandela's release begin.
- 1990—De Klerk announces Mandela's release. Ban on ANC, the PAC and the ban on media are lifted. Mandela refuses to give up the armed struggle, refuses to call for the lifting of international sanctions against South Africa until further progress is achieved and also refuses to accept an interim power-sharing arrangement proposed by the government.
- 1991—Negotiations on the transition continue marked by the release of hundreds of political prisoners. A new law allowed people to own land and property anywhere in the country irrespective of their race. The law assigning a racial group to every citizen is repealed and the world responds by lifting most sanctions against South Africa.
- On 7 July, 1991 the national conference elected Mandela as the president of the ANC. Mandela traveled to Cuba the same year and thanked Castro for extending a helping hand in their fight against apartheid.
- 1992—In a referendum, white South Africans vote for continuation of the reforms. Mandela divorces his wife Winnie.

- 1993—Conclusion of the negotiations on the transition agreeing upon the formation of a five year 'Government of National Unity' with a majority-rule constitution guaranteeing 'equality before the law and equal protection of the law', complete political rights, freedom of assembly and expression, and the right to 'choose a place of residence anywhere in the national territory'.

- Awarded the 1993 Nobel Peace Prize along with De Klerk.

- 1994—The ANC wins the countries' first all race elections securing around 63 per cent of the votes. On 9 May, 1994, the National Assembly unanimously elects Nelson Mandela as the President; De Klerk as one of the two deputy presidents.

- 1997—Mandela resigns as president of ANC. Travels to Libya to talk to Colonel Gaddafi to find a way to end UN sanctions imposed on South Africa in 1992.

- 1998—On his eightieth birthday, Nelson Mandela married Graca Machel, widow of Mozambican President.

- 1999—The ANC wins the general election. Mandela steps down from presidency to return to his birthplace. Is appointed by the UN to lead talks aimed at ending civil war in Burundi.

- 2002—Re-enters public life to stress upon the government to reorient its policy towards the AIDS crisis that had engulfed the country.

- 2003—Mandela officiates at a ceremony organized to mark the transfer of power in Burundi.

- 2004—Demise of Mandela's first wife. Mandela opens the Nelson Mandela Centre of Memory and Commemoration, an archive of his papers and records.
- 2005—His only surviving son dies of AIDS.
- 2007—Mandela celebrates his eighty ninth birthday. The occasion was marked with the launch of 'Elders', a group of eminent world leaders. His bronze statue was unveiled in London alongside that of Winston Churchill and Abraham Lincoln.
- 2008—The US officially removes ANC and Mandela from its terror watch list. Mandela speaks on the turmoil in Zimbabwe where President Mugabe uses violence and induces fear to stay in power.
- 2009—Mandela makes reappearance in politics to support Zuma, the ANC presidential candidate who later takes over as the third elected president of post apartheid South Africa.
- 2010—His birthday is declared as 'Nelson Mandela International Day' by the UN General assembly. Mandela celebrates his ninety second birthday.

Chapter 3
Childhood and Early Years

Nelson Mandela was born in Mvezo, a small village located in the district of Umtata, in the hills of Transkei, Africa on 18 July, 1918. He was named Rolihlahla Mandela–the prefix Nelson was added later. His original name means 'to pull a branch' or 'troublemaker' in common parlance. He is one of the thirteen children of his father's four wives and the youngest of four boys. Nelson had a peaceful childhood and most of the time was spent in cattle herding.

Nelson Mandela's place of birth is a splendid, remote part of South Africa but ridden with poverty. This is an area of high green hills with traditional green-painted huts overlooking the Bashee River in the valley below. His father, a local chief and the grandson of the king of the Xhosa-speaking Tembu people, controlled the area down to the river. The hut where Nelson Mandela was born is no longer there but a drive along a dirt track through the hills leads to where his father's Kraal (collection of huts) once stood.

In his childhood itself he migrated to another village, Qunu, where he would later build a house for himself. This is the place where he desires to be buried–in the family graveyard alongside his family members. Besides sheep rearing, he was also fond of stick fighting, a sport still popular in the rural areas of South Africa. According to one of his childhood friends, who still lives in Qunu, he would always fight to the bitter end. Mandela always made sure that he emerged as the winner even if the fight had to be carried forward the next day.

Coming from a royal family, Mandela was groomed to be much more than a cattle herder. On his father's demise, his custody went to his uncle, the head of his tribe, a rich and powerful man who sent him off to be educated in the court of the Regent, the acting Tembu king. Along with his mother, he had to undertake the long journey, on foot, to Mqhekezweni, the 'Great Place' where the Regent held court. Here, the young Mandela was treated as a member of the royal family. He lived in a hut with the Regent's son, and carefully watched the Regent as he presided over tribal meetings and managed to reach consensus between those with different views. Later, writing about his experience, Mandela said, 'one of the marks of a great chief is the ability to keep together all sections of his people...the Regent was able to carry the whole community because the court was representative of all shades of opinion'. In his political life, years later, as President, Mandela would try to achieve the same consensus within his cabinet. Watching the Regent at work was one of his first steps in becoming one of the world's greatest politicians.

Mandela's traditional roots and his royal privileges had a deep impact on his values and attitudes. He was greatly influenced by his African heritage including the rituals, the taboos and the elders telling stories of the bravery of his ancestors in defense of their fatherland during the wars. The seeds of the freedom struggle had already been sown.

Mandela was the first in his family to go to school. His primary education started at the age of seven in a Methodist missionary school, where he was given the name Mandela. His hobbies at school included boxing and running. He later studied in the all British Methodist College. It is here that his first encounter with ANC took place. He was expelled from college for helping to organize a strike against the white colonial rule of the institution.

Mandela ran away from home at the age of twenty three years to avoid an arranged marriage and moved to the south-western outskirts of Johannesburg. To make a living, he worked as a night watchman at a goldmine. Subsequently, he joined a law firm as an apprentice since he had already graduated in law from the University of South Africa.

The foster son of a Tembu chief, Mandela was raised in the traditional tribal culture of his ancestors, but at an early age learned the modern, inescapable reality of what came to be called apartheid, one of the most powerful and effective systems of oppression ever conceived. In classically elegant and absorbing prose, he tells of his early years as an impoverished student and law clerk in Johannesburg, of his slow political awakening, his central role in the rebirth of a stagnant ANC and the formation of its Youth League in the 1950s. He describes the struggle to reconcile his political activity with his devotion to his family, the anguished breakup of his first marriage, and the painful separation from his children.

Chapter 4
Marriage and Family

Mandela married thrice and has fathered six children and twenty grandchildren. He also has great-grandchildren. Mandela met his first wife, Evelyn Ntoko Mase in Johannesburg. She also happened to be from the Transkei area of South Africa. They had four children, two sons and two daughters. Their first daughter passed away at the age of nine months and the second daughter was named in her honor. Their marriage broke apart in 1957 after thirteen years. Mandela's frequent absence and commitment to revolutionary agitation was a catalyst in the divorce. His wife belonged to a faith that professed political neutrality. Their son was killed in a car crash in 1969 at the age of twenty five while Mandela was serving his prison sentence on Robben Island.

More recent reports (*The Times of India*–dated 9 August, 2010) quote his foundation and talk of a possibility of Nelson Mandela having fathered an illegitimate daughter following a brief affair in Cape Town in 1945. He was married for a year by this time and had a son from his first wife. This, of course is in the realm of speculation since substantive evidence like a DNA test is not available. Pule, who died last year had discovered from her grandmother who her father was. Her children are now continuing 'her battle for recognition as the seventh child fathered by the former apartheid-era freedom fighter' *(Daily Telegraph)*. Mandela's clan and his grandson have maintained that they had no intention of looking into the claim.

Mandela and Winnie

Mandela's second marriage was to Winnie Madikizela Mandela, a social worker. Two daughters were born to them. Later, Winnie was deeply torn by family discord which was a reflection of the turbulent political scenario. While her husband was serving a life sentence in Robben Island for terrorism and treason, her father became the agriculture minister in the Transkei. The separation took place in 1992 and they got divorced four years later. This also marked a political rift between the two.

The three decade long relationship with Winnie reveals Mandela's heart, mind and spirit. It is a story of two people, much in love with each other, torn apart by their differing political ambitions. "Mandela let us down. He agreed to a bad deal for the blacks. Economically, we are still on the outside...The economy is very much 'white'. It has a few token blacks, but so many who gave their life in the struggle have died unrewarded," said Madikizela-Mandela, in an interview published on www.standard.co.uk. All through, Mandela felt the guilt for all that Winnie had to endure and he tried to put up with her affairs and descent into violence. It so happened that Winnie and the children were his second love, the first being the ANC and struggle against apartheid.

Mandela announced his separation from Winnie in April 1992. The statement he made was a clear reflection of the tormenting experience. "I part from my wife with no recriminations. I embrace her with all the love and affection I have nursed for her inside and outside of prison from the moment I first met her." Some of his colleagues were of the opinion that Winnie was not on a favorable path and she would land up jeopardizing the liberation movement. There were political pressures and Mandela had to concede but the decision left scars that took some time to heal.

Mandela's daughter was married to the elder brother of King Mswati III of Swaziland while her father was still in prison. She was allowed to visit her father in prison by virtue of being married to a member of a reigning foreign dynasty. Other family members were denied access to Mandela.

Mandela himself remarried on his eightieth birthday in 1998. His third wife, Graca Machel is the widow of Samora

Machel, the former Mozambican president and ANC ally, killed in an air crash. The wedding was the culmination of months of international negotiations to set the bride-price to be remitted to her clan.

Since the time Mandela started to wage a battle against apartheid, it was evident that his wife had to be strong and brave. Some of his children never got to see Mandela since he was languishing in prison. When Thembi was killed in a car crash, Mandela was in prison and was not granted permission to attend his son's funeral. His other son, Makgatho, died of AIDS in 2005. One of his daughters from Winnie made history when she read out Nelson Mandela's address in 1985 refusing political pardon.

Chapter 5
Apartheid

Apartheid can be best described as a system of legal racial discrimination imposed by the whites in South Africa between 1948 and 1994. It was characterized by the minority rule of the white people and denial of rights of the indigenous people who happened to be in majority. Racial segregation existed since colonial times. The British colonial rulers had introduced a system of *Pass Laws* in the Cape Colony and Colony of Natal in the ninteenth century, restricting the movement of blacks into areas occupied by whites and colored people. This also restricted their movement from one district to another.

Apartheid, as an official policy, came into force with the general elections of 1948. People were classified into racial groups by the new legislation; residential areas were segregated, quite often by forced removals. There was discrimination when it came to education, medical care and other public services. From 1958 onwards, blacks were deprived of their citizenship. Legally, they could become citizens of one of the ten tribally based self-governing homelands called Bantustans.

A sign from the apartheid era

Racial Concentrations and Homelands

Racial concentrations of 30% or more by magisterial district

NOTE: Portions of Colored, Indian, and white areas may also have an equal or slightly larger percentage of other racial groups. Black areas have no other racial groups as high as 30%. Homelands are traditional areas set aside by the South African government for specific black ethnic groups. All have a black population in excess of 90%. Bophuthatswana, Transkei, and Venda have been granted nominal independence by South Africa.

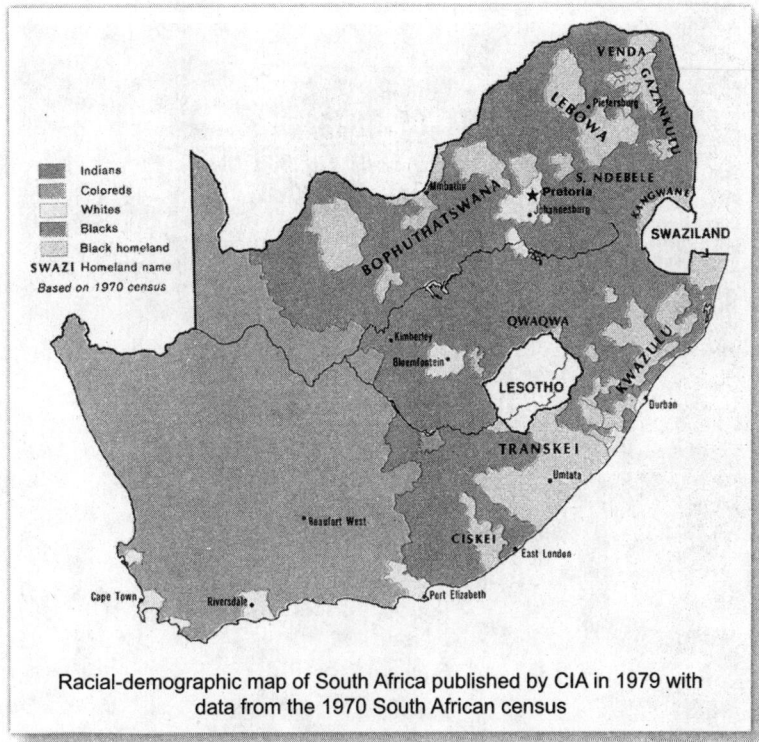

Racial-demographic map of South Africa published by CIA in 1979 with data from the 1970 South African census

The argument put forth by the National Party leaders were that South Africa does not comprise of a single nation but consisted of four distinct racial groups: white, black, colored and Indian, which were further divided into thirteen racial federations. The state passed laws paving way for 'grand apartheid' in addition to 'petty apartheid' laws which were aimed at institutionalizing racism. Some of the grand apartheid laws were the *Population Registration Act of 1950,* which formalized racial classification and introduced identity cards for everyone above eighteen years of age and the *Group Areas Act* which put an end to mixed residences and each race was allotted an area. This act also provided

'Petty apartheid': Sign on Durban beach in English, Afrikaans and Zulu (1989)

grounds for 'forced removals'. Under the homeland system, the South African government attempted to divide South Africa into a number of separate states, each of which was supposed to develop into a separate nation-state for a different ethnic group. Once a homeland was granted its nominal independence, its designated citizens had their South African citizenship revoked, replaced with citizenship of their homeland. The National Party passed a string of legislations which became known as 'petty apartheid'. The *Prohibition of Mixed Marriages Act of 1949* prohibited marriage between persons of different races, and the *Immorality Act of 1950* made sexual relations with a person of a different race a criminal offence. The *Reservation of Separate Amenities Act of 1953* assigned different spaces to people depending on their racial group in public places. In 1956, discrimination in employment was also formalized. The *Bantu Authorities Act of 1951* created separate government structures for the black citizens and was the first piece of legislation established to support the government's plan of separate development in the Bantustans. The parliament passed the *Separate Representation of Voters Act in 1956* transferring colored voters from the common voters' roll in the Cape to a new colored voters' roll.

Colored people were forced to live in separate townships, leaving their ancestral homes which had been occupied by their families for generations and received inferior education as compared to whites. They played an important role in the anti-apartheid movement for instance; the African Political Organization had an exclusive colored membership. The problem was compounded for women during apartheid since they had to suffer racial as well as gender discrimination. With almost no legal rights, no access to education and no right to own property, quite a few of the African women worked as agricultural or domestic workers for very low wages. Children suffered due to diseases related to malnutrition and bad hygiene, and the mortality rates were high. Families were separated as men who worked in urban areas were not allowed free movement due to pass laws.

Another minority in South Africa, the East Asian population, was difficult to define for the apartheid regime since it did not fit into any of the four designated racial groups. Chinese South Africans, whose ancestors came to work in the goldmines around Johannesburg in the late nineteenth century were classified as 'other Asians' whereas immigrants from Japan and Taiwan were considered 'honorary whites' with the same privileges owing to the diplomatic and trade relations which South Africa maintained with these countries.

In addition to apartheid, a program of social conservatism banning all the vices was undertaken. Media was strictly controlled and television was not introduced until 1976. Despite this, internal resistance to apartheid kept brewing and the government retaliated with police brutality. There were student protests, protests by the labor unions and around the same time, churches and church groups were emerging as crucial points of resistance. Majority of the whites supported apartheid but a small percentage continued to speak for egalitarianism and dignity of life.

Apartheid did not go unnoticed and was widely criticized by the international community. In his famous speech, *Wind of Change* in Cape Town, the then British Prime Minister, Harold Macmillan came out openly against apartheid. Che Guevara, speaking as Cuba's representative in 1964 in the United Nations said, "We speak out to put the world on guard against what is happening in South Africa. The brutal policy of apartheid is applied before the eyes of the nations of the world. The people of Africa are compelled to endure the fact that on the African continent, the superiority of one race over another remains an official policy, and that in the name of this racial superiority, murder is committed with impunity. Can the United Nations do nothing to stop this?" South Africa's racial policies continued to be a cause for concern but most countries in the UN felt that it was an internal affair and beyond UN's jurisdiction.

Nelson Mandela delivered a speech in the UN on apartheid immediately after his release in 1990. He said, "We feel especially honored and privileged to have the possibility today to stand at this particular place to speak to all of you who represent the peoples of the world… The tragedy is that what has created the need for this gathering and made it seem natural that we must gather in this historic meeting place is the fact of the continuing commission of a crime against humanity. How much better it would be–it would have been if we were meeting to celebrate a victory in hand, a dream fulfilled, the triumph of justice over a tyrannical past, the realization of the vision enshrined in the United Nations Charter and the Universal Declaration of Human Rights… We hold it as an inviolable principle that racism must be opposed by all the means that humanity has at his disposal."

With continued oppression, the United Nations General Assembly finally passed *Resolution 1761* condemning South African apartheid policies. In 1963, the United Nations Security Council passed *Resolution 181* calling for a voluntary arms embargo against South Africa, and in the same year, a Special Committee Against Apartheid was established to encourage and oversee plans of action against the regime. From 1964, the US and Britain discontinued their arms trade with South Africa. Economic sanctions were also debated and all cultural, educational and sporting interactions were severed. In 1978 and 1983, United Nations condemned South Africa at the World Conference Against Racism, and a significant disinvestment movement started, pressurizing investors to disinvest from South African companies or companies that did business with South Africa. Trade sanctions were imposed by the United States, United Kingdom and twenty three other countries in the late 1980's.

The Organization of African Unity (OAU) was created in 1963 with the prime objective to eradicate colonialism and improve social, political and economic condition of the blacks in South Africa. The organization criticized apartheid and demanded sanctions against South Africa. In 1969, fourteen nations from Central and East Africa gathered in Lusaka, Zambia to formulate the 'Lusaka Manifesto'. Although African leaders supported the emancipation of black South Africans, they recommended the use of peaceful means to attain this objective. The South African government rebuffed the Lusaka Manifesto and that forced the African countries to shift their strategy and adopt military means and resolve to severe talks with apartheid regime.

In 1966, B.J. Vorster was made the South African Prime Minister. He was not prepared to dismantle apartheid, but decided to follow an 'outward looking' policy to end South Africa's isolation and improve the reputation globally through 'dialogue' and 'détente'. International opposition to apartheid continued to grow but the Nordic countries, in particular, provided substantial moral and financial support. Sweden's Prime Minister, Olof Palme, a week before his assassination, addressed the Swedish People's Parliament Against Apartheid held in Stockholm. He declared, "Apartheid cannot be reformed; it has to be eliminated."

From 1985 to 1989, black townships became the focus of the struggle between anti-apartheid organizations and the Botha government, and serious political violence became a prominent feature of South Africa. Black townships had become almost ungovernable and numerous township councils were overthrown. Councillors, policemen and sometimes, even their families were attacked and murdered. Considering the situation, Botha declared a state of emergency in 1985 and thousands of people were detained under the Internal Security Act which had given sweeping powers to the police and military. Detention without trial became a common feature and media was censured. Most of the violence was directed towards the government but some incidents of deaths were reported as Inkatha and UDF-ANC factions clashed with each other. The state of emergency continued until 1990, when it was lifted by State President F W de Klerk.

Till 1960's, the situation appeared favorable for the apartheid regime. The country witnessed very high economic growth second only to that of Japan as investment was pouring in from the United States, France and Britain, resistance had been crushed and Mandela had been imprisoned on Robben Island.

In 1978, with Botha coming to power, the help extended by the Soviet Union to revolutionaries in South Africa and the sluggish economy had started to be a matter of great concern. It was noted that too much was being spent on the maintenance of separate homelands created for blacks. The poverty under which blacks lived made it practically impossible for them to make any kind of contribution to the economy of the country. The anti-apartheid movement was gaining momentum and international pressure was building up for the release of Mandela. The need to reform apartheid seemed inevitable and a new constitution was passed implementing a 'Tricameral Parliament' giving colored and Indians voting rights and parliamentary representation in separate houses–the House of Assembly for whites, the House of Representatives for colored and the House of Delegates for Indian. Each House dealt with laws pertaining to its racial group's own affairs which included education, health and other community issues. General matters like defense, industry taxation, etc. were handled by a cabinet having representatives from the three houses. Blacks were excluded from representation which meant that the majority had no say in decision making.

Mandela's increasing popularity forced the government to move him from Robben Island to a better location, allow more visitors including foreigners in order to give a boost to the international image and let the world know that Mandela was being treated well. Pass laws were abolished and black homelands were declared nation-states. Black labor unions were legitimized and property rights were granted to them in urban areas.

Mandela's release was conceded in 1985 subject to the ANC shunning violence for attaining their political objectives. Mandela's response which was read out by his daughter Zinzi pinned down the responsibility of violence on the apartheid regime saying that 'with democracy there would be no need of violence'. Finally, it was De Klerk who despite his initial conservative reputation as a conservative, proceeded with decisive negotiations aimed at ending the political stalemate in the country. As president, De Klerk took the step of repealing the discriminatory laws and lift the thirty year old ban on major anti-apartheid groups such as the African National Congress, the Pan–Africanist Congress, the South African Communist Party and the UDF. His reign was also marked by press freedom, suspension of death penalty and release of political prisoners including Nelson Mandela. An official apology was extended by De Klerk, "I apologize in my capacity as leader of the NP (National Party) to the millions who suffered wrenching disruption of forced removals; who suffered the shame of being arrested for pass law offences; who over the decades suffered the indignities and humiliation of racial discrimination."

Apartheid is a story of the bygone era but the remnants are still there lurking in the minds and hearts of the people. In an article, Robert Jensen, Journalism Professor at the University of Texas, very aptly said that apartheid is dead in South Africa but a new version of white supremacy lives on. The brutality ended with 1994 free elections but the white supremacist ideas and the racialized distribution of wealth didn't 'magically evaporate'.

But South Africans respect all cultures and that is definitely a hope generating factor. Apartheid is over and it is time to move ahead and acknowledge the fact that the problem of race is no longer political and requires cultural understanding and engagement. The diversity needs to be celebrated not abhorred. Racial harmony can be achieved by putting aside bitterness of the past and finding a common humanity.

Chapter 6
African National Congress

Presently led by Jacob Zuma, ANC was founded on 8 January, 1912 to fight for the rights of the black South African population. The founding of the ANC follows nearly three centuries of oppression of black South Africans by white South Africans and foreigners. The headquarters are in Johannesburg. The organization professes the ideology of socialism, democratic socialism and social democracy. The African National Congress has been South Africa's governing left-wing party, supported by its tripartite alliance with the Congress of South African Trade Unions (COSATU) and the South African Communist Party (SACP), since the establishment of non-racial democracy in April 1994. It defines itself as a 'disciplined force of the left'. The ANC considers itself as a force of national liberation in the post-apartheid era; it officially defines its umbrella agenda as the *National Democratic Revolution*. The National Democratic Revolution (NDR) is described as a process through which the National Democratic Society (NDS) is achieved; a society in which people are intellectually, socially, economically and politically empowered. The ANC is a member of the Socialist International. It also aims to redress socio-economic differences stemming from colonial and apartheid-era policies which discriminated against non-whites, such as land, housing and job distributions.

The military wing of ANC was founded in 1961 and was called the Umkhonto we Sizwe (Spear of the Nation). It has been the ruling party of South Africa since 1994. Following Zuma's accession to the ANC leadership in 2007 and Mbeki's resignation as president in 2008, the Mbeki faction of former ministers led by Mosiuoa Lekota split away from the ANC to form the *Congress of the People*.

The ANC flag is composed of three stripes: black, green and gold. The black symbolizes the people of South Africa who, for generations, have fought for freedom. The green represents the land, which sustained our people for centuries and from which they were removed by colonial and apartheid governments. The gold represents the mineral and other natural wealth of South Africa, which belongs to its entire people, but which has been used to benefit only a small racial minority. This flag was also the battle flag of the Umkhonto we Sizwe.

The government of the newly formed Union of South Africa began a systematic oppression of black people. With the Promulgation of Land Act in 1913, the blacks were pushed from their farms into the towns and cities to work, and their movement was restricted in South Africa. The ANC responded militarily to the attacks on the rights of the black people. The Youth League leaders, Nelson Mandela, Walter

The ANC Flag   The Logo

Sisulu and Oliver Tambo nurtured ideas based on African nationalism and were successful in involving masses into military struggles. They called for strikes, boycotts and other forms of defiance. The government reacted by banning party leaders and enacting new laws to prevent the situation from becoming more volatile. There were many acts of sabotage and military trainings for ANC members which continued in other countries. Involvement of students changed the dimensions of the struggle for national liberation, taking it to new heights. The government for the first time conceded in 1976 by enacting new reforms.

The ANC evolved to be the main challenge to the apartheid regime and played a vital role in resolving the conflict through actively participating in the peace making and peace building processes. The ANC negotiated the release of political prisoners and the indemnity from prosecution for returning exiles by agreeing to put an end to the existing climate of violence.

Mandela stood for the rights of his people and suffered all forms of repression during the fifties. He fought against the abuse of labor, making the Freedom Charter adopted by the Congress of the People in 1955 popular, fought against closing the open universities to black students and against the pass laws which controlled the movements of the colored people in the country. Mandela was not in favor of working with other racial groups to begin with but changed his position as the defiance movement, a campaign launched by the ANC against the unjust laws gathered momentum in 1952. Mandela traveled across the country to organize resistance and supported united action against the apartheid regime.

The Pretoria Minute was another significant step forward where agreements towards setting up an interim government and drafting a new constitution were reconsolidated in order to put a stop to direct violence in South Africa. However, violence continued and the trust between Mandela and De Klerk was violated.

Next step towards resolving the conflict was repealing the Population Registration Act which meant that no one could be deprived of rights on the basis of race. The result of these negotiations was an interim constitution that meant the transition from apartheid to democracy. A date was set for the first democratic elections on 27 April, 1994 in which the ANC emerged victorious securing 62.5 per cent of the votes.

Certain problems within the organization made it difficult for the ANC to achieve its objectives as desired and there were delays. There were corruption cases against some of its members relating to a series of bribes paid to companies involved in the R55 billion Arms Deal. Zuma is himself facing around 7813 charges relating to alleged fraud, bribery and corruption in the Arms Deal. The ANC went to the extent of abolishing the Scorpions, the multi-disciplinary agency that investigated and prosecuted organized crime and corruption and was heavily involved into investigating cases relating to Zuma and his legal advisor, Shaik. Other more recent corruption issues include sexual misconduct and criminal charges against the municipal manager of Beaufort West, Truman Prince and the Oilgate scandal in which huge funds were shifted to ANC from a state owned company. ANCs new National Executive Committee elected in 2007 had a large number of convicted criminals (post-apartheid) as its members. Winnie Mandela was convicted in the kidnapping of a fourteen year old boy.

ANC has been accused of using government resources and infrastructure against opposition parties like the Democratic Alliance. Over R1 billion of taxpayers' money was wasted over the past eight months on luxury vehicles, expensive hotels, banquets and other 'wasteful expenditures' which, if channeled properly could have built many homes and funded thousands of teachers.

Signs of dissent had started appearing within the ANC and acquired momentum in the party's 2007 national conference where the next president of ANC and in all probability, the next president of the country was to be selected. Mbeki bid for party leadership was challenged by Jacob Zuma, the former deputy president who was sacked by him on charges of corruption. Despite repeated allegations of wrong doing, which his supporters believe to be politically motivated, Zuma emerged as a popular candidate within the party and scored over Mbeki in one of the most contentious leadership battles in the history of ANC. Zuma's close ties with the South African Communist Party and the Congress of South African Trade Unions were a source of anxiety within the party. Despite being allies of the ANC, those groups seemed to be dominating the ANC under Zuma's leadership. The discord led to a breakaway and the establishment of a new party–Congress of the People (COPE) in 2008. Despite these challenges, ANC emerged victorious in the 2009 elections.

Chapter 7
The Sharpeville and Boipatong Massacres

Carrying the passes listing the name, birthplace, tribal affiliation, picture and a serial number had been like physical shackles for blacks for many decades. Moving without one gave the police license to haul him or her off to jail without giving any notice to the family or employer. For years, the system was hated and endured. The African National Congress had committed itself to a South Africa that belonged to all communities. By the late 1950's, a faction of the ANC had become disillusioned with the 'peaceful' methods and stood in opposition to the multi-racial future for South Africa. Known as Africanists, they formed an independent group in 1959, the Pan-Africanist Congress. Finally, the Pan-African Congress decided to address the issue, urging blacks to gather at local police stations peacefully without their passes, unarmed. People gathered in large numbers at Orlando township in the outskirts of Johannesburg led by Sobukwe, who headed the organization. Few arrests were made and the police opened fire killing three people and injuring twenty five.

On 16 March, 1960 Sobukwe wrote to the commissioner of police, Major General Rademeyer, stating that the PAC would be holding a five day, non-violent, disciplined and sustained protest campaign against pass laws starting on 21 March, 1960. At a press conference on 18 March, 1960 he further stated:

"I have appealed to the African people to make sure that this campaign is conducted in a spirit of absolute non-violence, and I am quite certain they will heed my call. If the other side so desires, we will provide them with an opportunity to demonstrate to the world how brutal they can be."

Everything appeared quiet at the Sharpeville police station, 28 miles south-west of Johannesburg but it was just the lull before the storm—the place was soon hitting the headlines across the globe. On 21 March, 1960, twenty policemen nervously saw the growing sea of humanity descending on the police station demanding arrest. Reinforcements had to be called and there was a blow-up. Firing started leading to stampede and many were shot in the back and killed in those awful two minutes. A few days before the massacre, a pamphlet was circulated in the nearby townships calling for people to stay away from work. Testimonies given point towards *'a degree of coercion of non-politicized Sharpeville residents who were pressurized into participating in the anti-pass protest'*. The police claimed that the first shot was fired in response to stone throwing by the crowd. The protesters continued to be shot at as they fled the location.

The Sharpeville massacre, as the event has become known, signaled the beginning of armed resistance in South Africa, and prompted worldwide condemnation of South Africa's apartheid policies.

The Sharpeville massacre of 21 March, 1960 is regarded by many as the defining moment in South Africa's struggle for liberation

The report submitted by Truth and Reconciliation Commission stated "The police deliberately opened fire on an unarmed crowd...and failed to facilitate access to medical and/or other assistance to those who were wounded...the Commission finds the former state and the minister of police directly responsible for the commission of gross human rights violations in that excessive force was unnecessarily used to stop a gathering of unarmed people."*

Sharpeville township in Sedibeng district hosts a memorial in honor of the victims of the 12 March, 1960

---

* Truth and Reconciliation Commission of South Africa Report, Volume 3, Chapter 6, October 1998.

massacre. The Sharpeville Memorial was officially opened on 21 March, 2002, and was erected to honor the victims of the Sharpeville Massacre in 1960 and all the freedom fighters in South Africa. The memorial is a symbol of hope and a pledge to the South Africans at large that an incident as horrific and painful as the Sharpeville massacre will never be allowed to happen again.

In 1966, the United Nations General Assembly proclaimed 21 March, the anniversary of the Sharpeville massacre, as the International Day for the Elimination of Racial Discrimination. In 1996, on the twenty sixth anniversary of the Sharpeville massacre, Nelson Mandela chose Sharpeville as the site to announce the signing of the new democratic constitution. The day is now commemorated as South Africa's Human Rights Day.

Boipatong township occupies an important place in the modern history of South Africa. Thirty people died overnight in June, 1992 in Boipatong that led to the signing of the Record of Understanding. Following the killings, the African National Congress suspended all bilateral talks with the then government of the National Party and the focus shifted to mass action.

The deadlock was finally broken on 26 September, 1992 when the NP and ANC signed the Record of Understanding that laid the basis for the structuring of the transition process, resumption of talks, with the parties agreeing on certain negotiation principles which included a need for a constituent assembly, an interim government of national unity, release of remaining political prisoners and curbing political violence amongst others.

These tragedies which happened to be some of the worst atrocities committed by the apartheid regime cannot and must not be forgotten. These killings exposed the ruthlessness of the old regime forcing the international community to condemn the massacres. It made the South Africans all the more determined to work towards change and forcing the De Klerk government to concede power to the majority. Sixteen years later, a democratic South Africa is basking in international glory after having hosted the best-ever World Cup. What needs to be done is to turn words into deeds by building a just and equitable society which will be a befitting homage to the martyrs of Sharpeville and Boipatong.

Chapter 8
Wind of Change

The British Prime Minister, Harold Macmillan was visiting the British colonies in Africa in the 1960. His address to the Parliament of South Africa, better known as the 'Wind of Change' speech signaled clearly that the Conservative controlled British government intended to grant independence to many of its territories—a phenomenon that the world subsequently witnessed in the successive years with the starting of the process of decolonization. It was a watershed moment in the struggle for Black Nationalism in Africa and the independence movement across the continent. The speech was named after the famous quotation used by Macmillan, "The wind of change is blowing through this continent. Whether we like it or not, this growth of national consciousness is a political fact." This was a repeat address—a similar one was delivered in Gold Coast, now Ghana. The words were of historical significance and indicated that the British had the good intention of working out a shift in policy with regard to apartheid. *"As a fellow member of the Commonwealth, it is our earnest desire to give South Africa our support and encouragement, but I hope you won't mind my saying frankly that there are some aspects of your policies which make it impossible for us to do this without being false to our own deep convictions about the political destinies of free men to which in our own territories we are trying to give effect."*

The speech did not come unanticipated as Macmillan had made it amply clear that he would take this chance of expressing his views clearly and openly on the political situation in South Africa. *"In the twentieth century, and especially since the end of the war, the processes which gave birth to the nation states of Europe have been repeated all over the world. We have seen the awakening of national consciousness in people who have for centuries lived in dependence upon some other power. Fifteen years ago this movement spread through Asia. Many countries there, of different races and civilizations, pressed their claim to an independent national life...Today the same thing is happening in Africa, and the most striking of all the impressions I have formed since I left London a month ago is of the strength of this African national consciousness. In different places it takes different forms, but it is happening everywhere... For its causes are to be found in the achievements of western civilization, in the pushing forward of the frontiers of knowledge, the applying of science to the service of human needs, in the expanding of food production, in the speeding and multiplying of the means of communication, and perhaps above all and more than anything else in the spread of education."*

Macmillan acknowledged the fact that the people of South Africa were rightly claiming self-rule and expressed the desire of taking up responsibility of creating as well as promoting egalitarian societies. The importance of the speech stems from the fact that it was the first public statement coming from Britain acknowledging Black Nationalist movements in South Africa. There was an immediate backlash against the speech from the right wing of the Conservative Party which supported imperialism and subsequent formation of a pressure group, the Conservative Monday Club.

Harold Macmillan's visit to South Africa always remained controversial. He received a frosty response from the apartheid regime for having spoken so frankly against the prevailing political system. Prime Minister Verwoerd responded by saying, "...*to do justice to all, does not only mean being just to the black man of Africa, but also to be just to the white man of Africa... it was white men who brought civilization to Africa, and that South Africa was bare (of people) when the first Europeans arrived.*" Verwoerd's response was applauded by the members of South Africa's parliament.

Chapter 9
The Arms Deal Saga

The first democratically elected government in South Africa decided to purchase US $ 4.6 billion worth of weapons which turned out to be the single largest and one of the most controversial public procurement deals in post-apartheid South Africa. This decision was the outcome of reviewing the South African defense forces whereby the need to re-equip and modernize the forces was stressed upon to meet the security needs of the fledgling democracy. This resulted in the proposal of a multi-billion rand Strategic Defense Procurement Package, widely referred to as the Arms Deal. The deal involved companies from Germany, Italy, Sweden, Britain, France and South Africa. The South African Department of Defense's Strategic Defense acquisition was to modernize its defense equipment, which included the purchase of corvettes, submarines, light utility helicopters, lead-in fighter trainers and advanced light fighter aircrafts.

Even though the government claimed that the deal will pay for itself in the long run through counter-trade agreements of investment in South Africa with contract companies. Known as the Offsets program, the massive expenditure involved kicked off a national debate on defense spending. Controversy surrounding the Arms Deal continued to spread as the allegations of irregularities and lack of transparency continued to be highlighted by the media.

The deal materialized at a time when Mandela was leaving office in 1999. At that time, South Africa was facing challenges posed by the various socio-economic problems like poverty, unemployment, HIV/AIDS among many others. Nelson Mandela and his then deputy allegedly knew far more about the behind-the-scenes negotiations in the build up to the Arms Deal, as well as some of the actions taken by Durban businessman, Schabir Shaik. Shaik and eleven of his companies are on trial in the Durban High Court on charges of corruption and fraud including the charge that Shaik asked for a bribe of R500 000 a year for two years, for Deputy President Jacob Zuma, from arms dealer Thomson. Investigations in South Africa and many other European countries probed the allegations of high level corruption involving top ANC leadership, including Jacob Zuma.

Jacob Zuma was charged with fraud, tax evasion and money laundering, and there seemed to be an intention to protect the country's likely to be president by dropping these charges, an act which would have spelt disaster for the democracy, the ANC and Zuma himself. The National Prosecuting Authority (NPA) would have been perceived to be buckling under political pressure. Justice was important in a country displaying excessive levels of crime and corruption. It would have also put a question mark on the moral fabric of the country and its ruling party.

Zuma consistently denied any wrong doing. As the drama unfolded, it was realized that billions of dollars were spent on defense equipment in a country where millions lived in poverty. It was also pointed out that there was no threat to the country's sovereignty and the spending was unjustified. In later stages, investigations focused on the conflict of interests, bribery and process violations.

In 2005, Zuma was sacked as South Africa's deputy president after his financial advisor, Shaik was convicted of fraud and corruption. Shaik was found guilty of trying to solicit a bribe from Thint (Thompson) of French Arms Company, Thales, on behalf of Zuma. In return, Zuma was to shield the firm from an investigation linked to the 1999 deal. The money was supposedly a donation to the Jacob Zuma Education Fund. The court judgement said there was evidence of 'a mutually beneficial symbiosis' between the two men, adding that the payments by Shaik to Mr Zuma 'can only have generated a sense of obligation in the recipient'. In 2006, Mr Zuma went on trial for corruption but the case collapsed after the prosecution said it was not ready to proceed more than a year after he was charged. Mr Zuma said he will quit as the ANC chief only if found guilty. His supporters maintained that he is a victim of a political smear campaign. The storm over South African multi-billion rand deal continued to rage. In November 2001, a three agency investigating team released its long awaited report.

Patricia de Lille, the president of the Independent Democrats, alleged in parliament that she had evidence of three payments by warship supplier Thyssen-Krupp on 29 January, 1999, each of R500,000 to the ANC, to the

Nelson Mandela Children's Fund and to the Community Development Foundation, a Mozambique charity associated with Mandela's wife, Graça Machel. The extent of involvement of Mandela and Mbeki had not been revealed before. The allegations are contained in the so-called 'secret', 260 page, KPMG, The State versus Schabir Shaik and others: Forensic Investigation (Draft Report on Our Factual Findings), dated 28 April, 2004.

Patricia explained her almost decade long efforts to expose the Arms Deal corruption and the latest action undertaken. "It has been a very long road for me, this Arms Deal saga. I was branded a 'useful idiot' and accused of telling 'blatant lies' in the months and years that followed my exposure of Arms Deal corruption, but I have stood by my guns. Now, after Tony Yengeni and Schabir Shaik's convictions, the chickens are slowly coming home to roost."

"Their convictions should be an example and warning to all South Africans that crime doesn't pay. However, throughout the Arms Deal saga I have never meant any ill towards individuals that have been accused and convicted, but have instead remained faithful to the cause of creating a South African identity and culture that is corruption-free. This is not for the purpose of pleasing the so-called First World, but rather to decimate specifically the negative impact their long and painful oppression has had on our societies and cultures."

The report says, "It is apparent that there was involvement at a high political level by Mbeki and Mandela to assist and advise on the eventual structuring of the share holding in African Defense Systems (ADS) (page 105)" and that "Mandela and Mbeki were involved in negotiations and discussions during the period leading to the day when the cabinet approved the list of bidders for supply in the Arms Deal." In the conclusions of the section dealing with Shaik's Arms Deal project, the report says, ". . . it appears that the involvement (of Mandela and Mbeki) was limited to . . . resolving disputes regarding the black empowerment partner component . . . (page 111)."

These and many other high profile cases were investigated by the Scorpions, the FBI-style unit independent of the South African Police. Incidentally, Scorpions are seen as the most effective crime-fighting unit in post-apartheid South Africa. Before Zuma was to go on trial, the ruling party under Jacob Zuma as the ANC president had demanded a disbanding of Scorpions in 2008.

Winnie Mandela, in an interview published in the London Evening Standard, bitterly lashed out at Nelson Mandela, saying that South Africa's first democratically elected president, who happened to be her ex-husband had become a 'corporate foundation' who was being 'wheeled out to collect the money'. Winnie Mandela believed that Nelson Mandela had no control over the ANC anymore and was just being used to get funds for the Nelson Mandela Foundation. "Look what they make him do. The great Mandela. He has no control or say any more. They put that huge statue of him right in the middle of the most affluent 'white' area of Johannesburg. Not here where we spilled our blood and where it all started...Mandela is now a corporate foundation. He is wheeled out globally to collect the money and he is content doing that. The ANC have effectively sidelined him but they keep him as a figurehead for the sake of appearance." She also criticized him for receiving the Nobel Prize along with De Klerk. "I cannot forgive him for going to receive the Nobel (Peace Prize in 1993) with his jailer F W de Klerk. Hand in hand they went."

Chapter 10
Nelson Mandela and Gandhi

The freedom struggle in the African continent was a reflection of Gandhian philosophy till the 1960's. Non-violence became the official position of most political parties and coalitions including the ANC which remained opposed to violence for the greater part of its existence. India was Gandhi's place of birth; South Africa his country of adoption and both countries contributed in shaping up his thoughts.

Writing in *Time Magazine* (3 January, 2000), Nelson Mandela wrote about Gandhi whom he considered as one of his teachers. The story was called '*The Sacred Warrior*'. "He dared to exhort non-violence in a time when the violence of Hiroshima and Nagasaki had exploded on us; he exhorted morality when science, technology and the capitalist order had made it redundant; he replaced self-interest with group interest without minimizing the importance of self. He is the archetypal anti-colonial revolutionary. His strategy of non-cooperation, his assertion that we can be dominated only if we cooperate with our dominators and his non-violent resistance inspired anti-colonial and anti-racist movements internationally in our century. Both Gandhi and I suffered colonial oppression, and both of us mobilized our respective people against governments that violated our freedoms... Gandhi remained committed to non-violence; I followed the Gandhian strategy for as long as I could, but then there came a point in our struggle when the brute force of the oppressor could no longer be countered through passive resistance alone. We founded Unkhonto we Sizwe and added a military dimension to our struggle. Even then, we chose sabotage because it did not involve the loss of life, and it offered the best hope for future race relations. Militant action became part of the African agenda officially supported by the Organization of African Unity (OAU) following my address to the Pan-African Freedom Movement of East and Central Africa (PAFMECA) in 1962, in which I stated, "Force is the only language the imperialists can hear, and no country became free without some sort of violence."

Arriving in South Africa at the age of twenty three years, Gandhi had an encounter with racism. 'The sight of wounded and whipped Zulus, mercilessly abandoned by their British persecutors, so appalled him that he turned a full circle from his admiration for all things British to celebrating the indigenous and ethnic'. He stayed on in South Africa to fight for human dignity and rights of the racially exploited. Gandhi did not rule out the use of violence altogether. He said, "Where choice is set between cowardice and violence, I would advise violence... I prefer to use arms in defense of honor rather than remain the vile witness of dishonor..."

Establishing the first anti-colonial political organization in South Africa (Natal Indian Congress), Gandhi threatened the apartheid government like no one else. During his twenty one years of stay in South Africa, Gandhi was imprisoned four times on his own insistence for deliberately breaching laws that discriminated against Indians and violated their dignity and freedom. In the initial stages, same strategy was adopted by the ANC till the brutality of the apartheid regime became unbearable. The prison conditions were extremely inhuman and changed slightly only in the 1980's, after Gandhi started exerting pressure on the government. Voicing his apprehensions on being convicted for the first time, Gandhi said, "Was I to be specially treated as a political prisoner? Was I to be separated from my fellow prisoners?" His approach was to accommodate to the prison conditions. As a satyagrahi, suffering in the path of freedom and justice was part of the life he had chosen. Mandela and his colleagues faced imprisonment in the cells of apartheid without any expectation of special privileges by virtue of being political prisoners. "We were never satyagrahis in that sense. We did not accept suffering, we reacted against it. I was as uncooperative on my first day of prison as I possibly could be. I refused to wear the prison shorts and I refused to eat the prison food. They gave me long trousers, and food that was somewhat more palatable, but at a heavy price. I was placed in solitary confinement where I discovered that human company was infinitely more valuable than any material advantage." Gandhi declined any favors offered to him exclusively but accepted improvements when these were shared with his fellow political prisoners. On Robben Island, Mandela observed the same principle.

Mandela considered Gandhi to be an extraordinary leader and divinely inspired. Gandhi believed that you can only be dominated if you decide to cooperate with the dominators. His strategies of non-cooperation and non-violence have inspired anti-colonial and anti-racial movements across the world.

Both Gandhi and Mandela witnessed and suffered colonial repression and successfully managed to mobilize the masses to fight for freedom. Mandela continued to follow Gandhi for a long time till there came a point when the "brute force of the oppressor could not be countered through passive resistance alone...we founded Unkhonto we Sizwe and added a military dimension to our struggle, choosing sabotage since it did not involve loss of life... Militant action became part of the African agenda officially supported by the Organization of African Unity (OAU) following my address to the Pan-African Freedom Movement of East and Central Africa (PAFMECA) in 1962, in which I stated, "Force is the only language the imperialists can hear, and no country became free without some sort of violence."—Nelson Mandela (the sacred warrior). Violence and non-violence are not mutually exclusive; it is the predominance of the one or the other that labels a struggle.

Rejecting the popular belief that poverty can be eliminated by sheer hard work and Adam Smith's notion of human nature as motivated by self-interest and basic needs, Gandhi reminded us that we have a moral and spiritual dimension by evoking non-violence, justice and equality. He identified with the masses and believed that economic equality will not become a reality unless one reduces oneself to the level of the poorest of the poor. Satyagraha was waged to transform and not to destroy the oppressor.

Gandhi remained critical of advanced industrial society giving priority to right to work as opposed to mechanization which had led to concentration of wealth in the hands of the few and denied access of opportunity to the masses. As many countries find themselves in difficult situations with economic crisis and people starving, we are forced to consider the Gandhian alternative. "At a time when Freud was liberating sex, Gandhi was reining it in; when Marx was pitting worker against capitalist, Gandhi was reconciling them; when the dominant European thought had dropped God and soul out of the social reckoning, he was centralizing society in God and soul; at a time when the colonized had ceased to think and control, he dared to think and control; and when the ideologies of the colonized had virtually disappeared, he revived them and empowered them with a potency that liberated and redeemed." Gandhi and Mandela, both suffered for a cause. "Though separated in time, there remains a bond between us, in our shared prison experiences, our defiance of unjust laws and in the fact that violence threatens our aspirations for peace and reconciliation." — Nelson Mandela

The most distinguished and popular victories of the twentieth century were in India, the US and South Africa making those leaders heroes of human civilization. Mahatma Gandhi continued to be a source of inspiration for Mandela in facing adversity with dignity. While Gandhi's approach emphasized heightened spiritual awareness as a means of transforming the Indian people, Mandela's was, in later stages, a more militant form of social protest which succeeded in stimulating the political energy of South

Africa's black majority. "By that time the demands of our people were loud, persistent and clear: all our efforts as a people, the whole record of relentless struggle under the leadership of the African National Congress, were being met with ever-increasing violence and repression by the racist state. The time had arrived when we needed to reinforce our mass political action with the hammer blows of an armed struggle."

Chapter 11
The Shifting Sands of Illusion

In June 1953, Nelson Mandela wrote an article for the monthly Journal, *Liberation*, titled *The Shifting Sands of Illusion,* in which he outlined the ANC's response to the formation of the Liberal Party which was a group of liberal minded anti-apartheid, non-racial people.

The Liberal Party constitution professed to uphold the 'essential dignity of every human being irrespective of race, color or creed, and the maintenance of his fundamental rights'. Mandela felt that the new party was speaking more in terms of broad generalizations with no practical application in the South African context. The only explicit statement coming from them was 'that political rights based on a common franchise roll be extended to all *suitably qualified* persons' which went against the democratic principle of 'one adult, one vote'. The ANC and its allies stood for votes for all and that was the point of departure. "In South Africa, where the entire population is almost split into two hostile

camps in consequence of the policy of racial discrimination, and where recent political events have made the struggle between oppressors and oppressed more acute, there can be no middle course. The fault of the Liberals–and this spells their doom–is to attempt to strike just such a course. They believe in criticizing and condemning the government for its reactionary policies but they are afraid to identify themselves with the people and to assume the task of mobilizing that social force capable of lifting the struggle to higher levels."
–Nelson Mandela

The Liberals wanted to restrict the means of struggle within democratic and constitutional parameters and oppose all forms of totalitarianism such as communism and fascism but Mandela felt that 'these means can only have a basis in reality for those people who enjoy democratic and constitutional rights'. The reality in South Africa made it clear that no victory could be won without desperate resistance from the government and the struggle will take the form of bitter resistance by the oppressed for the overthrow of racial discrimination. "The theory that we can sit with folded arms and wait for a future parliament to legislate for the 'essential dignity of every human being irrespective of race, color or creed' is crass perversion of elementary principles of political struggle. No organization whose interests are identical with those of the toiling masses will advocate conciliation to win its demands."

The proposal to adhere to constitutional means of struggle in the South African context meant giving in to the laws made by the minority which was in the mode of denial of democracy. It meant obeying the laws which debar the majority from participating in the democratic processes of the government. The real question was–in the general struggle for political rights, can the oppressed people count on the Liberal Party as an ally? The new party, Mandela said, merely gave organizational expression to a tendency which had existed for many years among a section of the white ruling class which hates and is fearful of the idea of a revolutionary democracy in South Africa. "The high-sounding principles enunciated by the Liberal Party, though apparently democratic and progressive in form, are essentially reactionary in content. They stand not for the freedom of the people but for the adoption of more subtle systems of oppression and exploitation. Though they talk of liberty and human dignity, they are subordinate henchmen of the ruling circles. They stand for the retention of the cheap labor system and of the subordinate colonial status of the non-European masses together with the Nationalist Government whose class interests are identical with theirs. In practice they acquiesce in the slavery of the people, low wages, mass unemployment, the squalid tenements in the locations and shanty-towns."

"We, of the non-European liberation movement are not racialists. We are convinced that there are thousands of honest democrats among the white population who are prepared to take up a firm and courageous stand for unconditional equality, for the complete renunciation of 'white supremacy'. To them we extend the hand of sincere friendship and brotherly alliance. But no true alliance can be built on the shifting sands of evasions, illusions and opportunism. We insist on presenting the conditions which make it reasonable to fight for freedom. The only sure road to this goal leads through the uncompromising and determined mass struggle for the overthrow of fascism and the establishment of democratic forms of government."

In his presidential address in 1953, better known as *'No Easy Walk to Freedom',* Mandela talked about how, since 1912, the African people have discussed the shameful misdeeds of those who rule the country. "Year after year, they have raised their voices in condemnation of the grinding poverty of the people, the low wages, the acute shortage of land, the inhuman exploitation and the whole policy of white domination. But instead of more freedom, repression began to grow in volume and intensity, and it seemed that all their sacrifices would end up in smoke and dust. Today the entire country knows that their labors were not in vain, for a new spirit and new ideas have gripped our people. Today the people speak the language of action: there is a mighty awakening among the men and women of our country and the year 1952 stands out as the year of this upsurge of national consciousness."

In June 1952, the African National Congress and the South African Congress took the plunge and launched the Campaign for the Defiance of Unjust Laws. The agitation proved to be a strong social force and an effective way to generate political awareness amongst the masses. "The entire country was transformed into battle zones where the forces of liberation were locked up in immortal conflict against those of reaction and evil. Our flag flew in every battlefield and thousands of our countrymen rallied around it. We held the initiative and the forces of freedom were advancing on all fronts. It was against this background and at the height of this campaign that we held our last annual provincial conference in Pretoria from the 10 to 12 of October last year. In a way, that conference was a welcome reception of those who had returned from the battlefields and a farewell to those who were still going to action. The spirit of defiance and action dominated the entire conference." The government retaliated and many people were arrested, tried and convicted for participating in the Defiance Campaign. Almost immediately, the Criminal Laws Amendment Act was passed which provided heavy penalties for the convicts including whipping of defiers, even women.

A new situation was created by these measures and the ANC was forced to review its strategy by pausing to make plans to overcome dangers. "Long speeches, the shaking of fists, the banging of tables, and strongly worded resolutions out of touch with the objective conditions do not bring about mass action and can do a great deal of harm to the organization and the struggle we serve. The masses had to be prepared and made ready for new forms of political struggle." The movement had to be revived, and a fresh and more powerful offensive had to be launched against the enemy. The crackdown had virtually disabled the circulation of leaflets and all other publicity carried out prior to Suppression of Communism Act and similar other measures. The apartheid regime, alarmed at the resolute rise of national consciousness was doing everything in its capacity to crush all opposition.

Meanwhile, the living conditions of the masses, which were already difficult, continued to further deteriorate. More and more were getting poorer by the day, not having enough resources to feed their families. People were denied the right to security in the event of unemployment or any other emergency. Lack of medical facilities left the population ravaged by dreaded diseases. *"You will also recall the story of human beings toiling pathetically from the early hours of the morning till sunset, fed only on mealie meal served on filthy sacks spread on the ground and eating with their airy hands. People falling ill and never once being given medical attention. You will also recap the revolting story of a farmer who was convicted for tying a laborer by his feet from a tree and had him flogged to death, pouring boiling water into his mouth whenever he cried for water. These things which have long vanished from many parts of the world still flourish in South Africa today. None will deny that they constitute a serious challenge to Congress and we are duty bound to find an effective remedy for these obnoxious practices."*

The government had introduced the Native Labor (Settlement of Disputes) Bill and the Bantu Education Bill. The aim was to destroy all trade unions which were fighting for the rights of the workers. The Minister of Native Affairs, Verwoerd, had also been brutally clear in explaining the objects of the Bantu Education Bill. According to him, the aim of this law is to teach our children that Africans are inferior to Europeans. African education would be taken out of the hands of people who taught equality between black and white. "It might well be that the children of those who criticize the government and who fight its policies will almost certainly be taught how to drill rocks in the mines and how to plough potatoes on the farms of Bethal. High education might well be the privilege of those children whose families have a tradition of collaboration with the ruling circles."

These bills were outrightly rejected and condemned by the ANC and this affirmed its firm belief in the principles set forth in the Universal Declaration of Human Rights. These were—everyone has the right to education; that education shall be directed to the full development of human personality and to the strengthening of respect for human rights and fundamental freedoms.

It shall promote understanding, tolerance and friendship among the nations, racial or religious groups and shall further the activities of the United Nations for the maintenance of peace. That a parent has the right to choose the kind of education that shall be given to their children. The attitude of the government, Mandela said is "Let's beat them down with guns and batons, and trample them under our feet. We must be ready to drown the whole country in blood if only there is the slightest chance of preserving white supremacy."

The entire continent of Africa had started seething with discontent and was witnessing powerful revolutionary eruptions. "The day of reckoning between the forces of freedom and those of reaction is not very far off. I have not the slightest doubt that when that day comes, truth and justice will prevail…the feelings of the oppressed people have never been more bitter."

Chapter 12
The Trials

Treason Trial

Almost the entire executive of the African National Congress, Congress of Democrats, South African Indian Congress, Colored People's Congress and the South African Congress of Trade Unions were arrested in response to the adoption of the Freedom Charter. The charges were 'high treason and a countrywide conspiracy to use violence to overthrow the present government and replace it with a communist state' and the legally prescribed punishment for high treason was death.

The accused were backed up by a legal team and a fund was set up to pay for the bail of the accused. The trial proceeded in two stages; a preparatory examination to find out if there is sufficient evidence to support a trial and subsequently, a trial by the Supreme Court. The government collected over 12,000 items of documentation, over a period of three years. The prosecution made an attempt to prove that the Freedom Charter was tilted towards communism but this was declared as a fallacy and the regime admitted that the Charter was 'a humanitarian document that might well represent the natural reaction and aspirations of non-whites to the harsh conditions in South Africa'.

It took just about a week of the trial for most charges to be dropped. However, a new indictment was issued against thirty people from the ANC. Nelson Mandela and Walter Sisulu was among the finally accused. The trial proved to be a serious blow to the ANC and the other members of the Congress Alliance. In his biography, Nelson Mandela suggests that the Treason Trial verdict pushed the South African government into a new level of conflict with anti-apartheid organizations: *"During the Treason Trial, there were no examples of individuals being isolated, beaten and tortured in order to elicit information. All of those things became common place shortly thereafter."*

Mandela was asked by the prosecution during the trial if their demand for freedom reflected an anti-white sentiment. Mandela replied that they were not against whites but were opposed to white supremacy and were being supported by some sections of Europeans in their struggle against apartheid. During the period of the Treason Trial, the National Party won another election, ANC and PAC were declared illegal (under the Suppression of Communism Act), the South African government held a referendum (whites only, of course) on the question of whether South Africa should become a republic, and the PAC initiated anti-pass demonstrations, one of which ended up as the Sharpeville massacre. Nelson Mandela, Walter Sisulu and six others were eventually given a life sentence for treason in 1964 at what is known as the Rivonia Trial.

The Rivonia Trial

The process of transition from apartheid to democracy in South Africa is almost unthinkable without Mandela. There was a possibility of death sentence being served on Mandela along with some of his colleagues in 1964 in the Rivonia Trial. The threat was very real. It was almost certain that Verwoerd, the then prime minister and architect of apartheid would do everything in his capacity to carry out the death sentence.

The Rivonia Trial took place in South Africa between 1963 and 1964 in which ten leaders of the African National Congress, including Nelson Mandela were tried for 221 acts of sabotage to overthrow the apartheid system. Rivonia is a suburb of Johannesburg. These leaders had moved to a privately owned farm from where all their activities were coordinated. They were arrested on charges of violence, sabotage and treason. Once the prosecution had outlined its case, the defense team was faced with the formidable task of waging 'a battle to prevent the death sentence being carried out'. For Mandela it was an opportunity for political offensive and not a case of straight legal defense and he wanted to use the courtroom to explain and highlight what they were aiming to do and why. There was no possibility of denials of guilt which was tantamount to their signing their own death sentence. The defense team was indeed faced with a complex situation. The accused had taken a prior decision that even while giving evidence under oath, 'they would state the facts as fully as possible but would not under any circumstances reveal any information whatsoever about their organizations or about people involved in the movement, where such information could in any way endanger their liberty'. This, the defense team feared would antagonize the judges.

The prosecution definitely started with all the advantages. Its strategy not to charge the accused with high treason but under the Sabotage Act removed a great deal of the onus of proof from the prosecution and placed it on the defense. Throughout the trial, the judge responded to the needs of the whites and the right wing consistently called for the death penalty. *The Star* welcomed the life sentences as a lesson to anyone wanting to overthrow the existing order. The defense team was not interviewed by the media at all. The government was determined to continue with the reign of terror and crush all opposition and resistance.

The trial was condemned by the United Nations Security Council and nations across the globe which resulted in international sanctions against the South African government in certain areas. Originally, a death penalty had been requested, but the apartheid regime changed its stance due to growing international pressure and worldwide protests. Speaking at the dock of the Pretoria Supreme Court in June 1964, Mandela said, "This is the struggle of the African people, inspired by their own suffering and experience. It is a struggle for the right to live. I have cherished the ideal of a democratic and free society, in which all persons live together in harmony and with equal opportunity. It is an ideal which I hope to live for and achieve. But, if needs be, my Lord, it is an ideal for which I am prepared to die."

He continued, "I am the First Accused. I hold a Bachelor's Degree in Arts and practiced as an attorney in Johannesburg for a number of years in partnership with Oliver Tambo. I am a convicted prisoner serving five years for leaving the country without a permit and for inciting people to go on strike at the end of May 1961.

At the outset, I want to say that the suggestion made by the State in its opening that the struggle in South Africa is under the influence of foreigners or communists is wholly incorrect. I have done whatever I did, both as an individual and as a leader of my people, because of my experience in South Africa and my own proudly felt African background, and not because of what any outsider might have said.

In my youth in the Transkei, I listened to the elders of my tribe telling stories of the old days. Amongst the tales they related to me were those of wars fought by our ancestors in defence of the fatherland. The names of Dingane and Bambata, Hintsa and Makana, Squngthi and Dalasile, Moshoeshoe and Sekhukhuni, were praised as the glory of the entire African nation. I hoped then that life might offer me the opportunity to serve my people and make my own humble contribution to their freedom struggle. This is what has motivated me in all that I have done in relation to the charges made against me in this case.

Having said this, I must deal immediately and at some length with the question of violence. Some of the things so far told to the Court are true and some are untrue. I do not, however, deny that I planned sabotage. I did not plan it in a spirit of recklessness, nor because I have any love of violence. I planned it as a result of a calm and sober assessment of the political situation that had arisen after many years of tyranny, exploitation and oppression of my people by the whites.

I admit immediately that I was one of the persons who helped to form Umkhonto we Sizwe, and that I played a prominent role in its affairs until I was arrested in August 1962.

In the statement which I am about to make I shall correct certain false impressions which have been created by State witnesses. Amongst other things, I will demonstrate that certain of the acts referred to in the evidence were not and could not have been committed by Umkhonto. I will also deal with the relationship between the African National Congress and Umkhonto, and with the part which I personally have played in the affairs of both organizations. I shall deal also with the part played by the Communist Party. In order to explain these matters properly, I will have to explain what Umkhonto set out to achieve; what methods it prescribed for the achievement of these objects, and why these methods were chosen. I will also have to explain how I became involved in the activities of these organizations... Firstly, we believed that as a result of government policy, violence by the African people had become inevitable, and that unless responsible leadership was given to canalize and control the feelings of our people, there would be outbreaks of terrorism which would produce an intensity of bitterness and hostility between the various races of this country which is not produced even by war. Secondly, we felt that without violence there would be no way open to the African people to succeed in their struggle against the principle of white supremacy. All lawful modes of expressing opposition to this principle had been closed by legislation, and we were placed in a position in which we had either to accept a permanent state of inferiority, or to defy the government. We chose to defy the law. We first broke the law in a way which avoided any recourse to violence; when this form was legislated against, and then the government resorted to a show of force to crush opposition to its policies, only then did we decide to answer violence with violence…who will deny that thirty years of my life have been spent knocking in vain, patiently, moderately and modestly at a closed and barred door? What have been the fruits of moderation? The past thirty years have seen the greatest number of laws restricting our rights and progress, until today we have reached a stage where we have almost no rights at all."

"At the beginning of June 1961, after a long and anxious assessment of the South African situation, I, and some colleagues, came to the conclusion that as violence in this country was inevitable, it would be unrealistic and wrong for African leaders to continue preaching peace and non-violence at a time when the government met our peaceful demands with force…This conclusion was not easily arrived at. It was only when all else had failed, when all channels of peaceful protest had been barred to us, that the decision was made to embark on violent forms of political struggle, and to form Umkhonto we Sizwe. We did so not because we desired such a course, but solely because the government had left us with no other choice." The Manifesto of Umkhonto published on 16 December, 1961 stated:"The time comes in the life of any nation when there remain only two choices – submit or fight. That time has now come to South Africa. We shall not submit and we have no choice but to hit back by all means in our power in defense of our people, our future and our freedom."

Mandela claimed that the struggle was funded from internal sources and only in rare instances like the Treason Trial, help came from sympathizers abroad. "Our fight is against real and not imaginary, hardships or, to use the language of the State Prosecutor, 'so-called hardships'. Basically, we fight against two features which are the hallmarks of African life in South Africa and which are entrenched by legislation which we seek to have repealed. These features are poverty and lack of human dignity, and we do not need communists or so-called 'agitators' to teach us about these things... Poverty goes hand in hand with malnutrition and disease. The incidence of malnutrition and deficiency diseases is very high amongst Africans. Tuberculosis, pellagra, kwashiorkor, gastroenteritis, and scurvy bring death and destruction of health. The incidence of infant mortality is one of the highest in the world...the present government has always sought to hamper Africans in their search for education...all the better jobs of the industry are reserved for whites...above all, we want equal political rights because without them our disabilities will be permanent."

On 11 June, 1964, at the conclusion of the trial, Mandela and seven others were convicted. Mandela was found guilty on four charges of sabotage and along with others was sentenced to life imprisonment. Mandela spent nearly three decades in prison as a result of the trial and was finally released in February 1990 by President FW de Klerk. While Mandela was serving the sentence, his reputation as the most effective leader of anti-apartheid movement was gaining ground outside. Mandela regarded himself as an African patriot who saw a classless society as an ideal one. Even tribal societies, he elaborated, had no distinction between the rich and the poor, they were devoid of exploitation and the means of production belonged to the tribe. Mandela admitted to being influenced by Marxist thought and accepted the need for some kind of socialism to enable people to break the vicious cycle of poverty. But contrary to the Marxists criticism and discarding of the parliamentary system, he admired the democratic system and believed the British parliament to be the most democratic institution in the world.

Lockerbie Trial

On 21 December, 1988, Panam flight 103 crashed at the Scottish town of Lockerbie killing 270 people on board. The cause was identified as sabotage and two Libyans were accused and finally indicted after trial in November 1991. President Mandela took an active and keen interest in resolving the dispute between Libya on one hand and the United States and Britain on the other over bringing the two suspects to trial. Informal discussions were held with President Bush over the proposal that these two Libyans be tried in a third country which met with favorable response from Bush as well as President Mitterrand of France and King Juan Carlos I of Spain. The venue was finalized as South Africa for the Panam flight 103 bombing trial. Due to apprehensions and lack of confidence in foreign courts expressed by the then British Prime Minister John Major, the trial was delayed by three years despite Mandela's warning that "No one nation should be complainant, prosecutor and judge."

A compromise was worked out and a decision was taken to hold the trial in the Netherlands guided by Scots law. President Mandela negotiated the handover of the two accused with Colonel Gaddafi. The trial took nine months, verdict was announced in 2001 with one of the accused (Megrahi) being convicted and sentenced to twenty seven years of imprisonment in a Scottish jail. The trial featured the testimonies of 235 witnesses and pieces of thousands of physical and documentary evidence recovered from the wreckage of the plane and crucial witnesses from the US, Switzerland, Malta and Sweden.

The murder conviction of al-Megrahi was based on four findings—he was proved to be a Libyan intelligence officer 'of fairly high rank', he dealt with military procurement and was identified as the purchaser of the clothing found in the bomb suitcase. The court stated: "The clear inference which we draw from this evidence is that the conception, planning and execution of the plot which led to the planting of the explosive device was of Libyan origin." The court did not, however, indicate how high up the Libyan government chain of command the responsibility extends, nor did it rule out the possibility that Iran had also been involved in the bombing plot, as many experts still suspect.

A large number of people expected Libya to make an ex-gratia payment to the families of the accused as part of the multi-billion dollar law suit settlement and to meet the conditions set by President George Bush for lifting US sanctions against Libya. Libya was expected to 'accept responsibility for this act and compensate the families'. Despite the mixed verdict and limited evidence, the Lockerbie trial apparently succeeded in breaking the vicious cycle of violence between the US and Libya with Libya agreeing to withdraw its support to terrorist groups, thereby contributing to international peace and security.

Mandela visited Megrahi in jail and recommended that he be shifted to a country where he can be visited by his family and friends and not forced to spend such a long time in solitary confinement. Megrahi was moved to Greenock jail and out of solitary confinement he was finally released and allowed to return to Libya on compassionate grounds since he was diagnosed with cancer and had only a couple of months to live. His release was precipitated due to support and recommendation extended by the Nelson Mandela Foundation in a letter sent to the Scottish government.

Chapter 13
The Prison Years

In the winter of 1964, Nelson Mandela arrived on Robben Island. Here he was confined to a small cell where he had to sleep on the floor, use a bucket for a toilet and do hard labor in a quarry. As a D-group prisoner, which is the lowest category, he had to live with very basic conditions. Mandela spent eighteen out of twenty seven years of prison life here. It is here that Mandela matured into a leader with his dignified defiance and won one of the greatest political battles that created a new democratic South Africa.

Nelson Mandela's cell on Robben Island

Nelson Mandela's prison cell

Prisoners crushing rocks at Robben Island

The above footage was taken by a South African government cameraman in 1977, showing Mandela working with other prisoners on a road repair. By this time, Mandela was a near forgotten man–he had been on Robben Island for thirteen years and his words were banned throughout the country.

From Robben Island, from 1976-79, Mandela wrote letters to his wife confessing his love for her and the painful guilt he felt for her and his family since it was the political cause that came first in his life. In *'The Dark Years'* in his autobiography, Mandela described the harsh daily routine during his years on Robben Island. In the prison, the day started at 5:30 each morning but the prisoners were allowed to come out of the cells only at 6:45. "This was one moment in those early days when we could have a whispered word with our colleagues. The warders did not like to linger while we cleaned, so it was a chance to talk softly...Like everything else in prison, diet is discriminatory. In general, colored and Indians received a slightly better diet than Africans."

Neville Alexander, one of the young revolutionaries and fellow prisoner on Robben Island, recounted how Mandela's traits of character were revealed in his dealings with the authorities and fellow prisoners. The first time he met Mandela was in what was called the isolation section and as the familiarity grew, the warmth and the genuine interest which was very much part of the man, emerged. Gradually they came to understand that in terms of the strategic vision that Mandela and his friends nurtured, there was consistency and belief in principled success. One of the few occasions that affected him deeply was the death of his son and regular reports of his wife's liaison with other men for which he took the blame on himself.

In jail, Mandela read literature, poetry, etc. in later years but most of the period was confined to political, historical and legal matters. 'He read very deeply, but not very widely' and greatly enjoyed reading biographies. He displayed substantial knowledge of colonial and pre-colonial history in terms of oral tradition.

Neville Alexander said that Mandela can be stubborn. "I have always experienced that stubbornness more as a kind of arrogance, as an unwillingness to accept something which questions a cherished notion of his...He always made the point. If they say you must run, insist on walking slowly. That was the whole point. We are going to set the terms."

Jack Swart, who became Mandela's chef when he was moved to Victor Verster Prison in 1988, provided glimpses of private times in his life including visits from his family, wife and colleagues. The first guest who came for a meal with him was of course, Winnie who visited him quite often in jail. On Christmas, she brought little presents for everyone but the staff had to return them since they were not allowed to accept any gifts from prisoners or their families. Swart described relations between Mandela and Winnie as quite good until the Stompie incident after which her visits became infrequent.

In Robben Island, Mandela and his friends were addressed as 'The Rivonians'. The other prisoners always went to him in case of problems, seeking his advice or expecting him to represent on their behalf. That time no one anticipated that prisoner Mandela would one day emerge from the prison to become the president of South Africa.

Fixile Bam was on Robben Island with Mandela for ten years and narrated stories of his political skills and his effort to learn the African language in prison. Even though Mandela was imprisoned, he was preparing for leadership outside. He was very serious about Africans, not just the people but their thought processes also. Mandela believed that African belonged to the soil and any political solution had to involve them. Although he had been sentenced to life imprisonment, a condition of survival in prison was to believe that victory will finally come and the struggle would be successful in the end. Mandela nurtured the belief that freedom will be theirs during their lifetime and that he would play a definite role in winning the war of liberation. Mandela, all these years was also consciously preparing himself for a liberated South Africa in which people would have to be developed in terms of their skills and be socially and economically liberated in real terms.

In prison, he played the role of reconciliation between different groups, primarily between the PAC and ANC and also in the unity movement later. It was a conciliatory and consultative initiative to form the Prisoner's Committee to look after the interests of prisoners, irrespective of their political affiliations. Mandela happened to be a great story teller and often interspersed his conversations with these stories. He talked about his mistakes without reservation and laughed at himself. Mandela had a great deal of knowledge about people and took a lot of interest in people at all levels.

He is a much disciplined person in small things as in big ones and never wanted to be given favors which other people could not have.

Mandela did become emotional sometimes—it was not all strength. When he heard about the death of his mother, he was quite withdrawn for a day and did not even talk to anyone. Another vulnerability was his tendency to trust people too much, even those who did not deserve that trust. One thing Mandela cannot tolerate is betrayal.

George Bizo, Mandela's lawyer and constant visitor during his imprisonment, said that Mandela was clear that he will be serving a long prison term. The process of decolonization in the rest of Africa was an encouraging factor but Mandela knew that the whites will hold on as long as they could. One thing he did not do was to express a feeling of despair which would have been counter-productive to the struggle.

They were generally kept in the dark about what was happening in the outside world. Even when they were allowed to get newspapers and magazines, practically everything that had to do with national or international politics was cut out. "The silence was deafening to them and they were very hungry for information."

Legal consultations were carried out with utmost caution–it was almost certain that the consultation rooms were bugged. The 80's saw many temptations being extended to Mandela for instance, exchanging his freedom for abandoning the armed struggle. The apartheid government believed that they could bribe Mandela in the same manner in which they had bribed the Bantustan leaders. This is why they gave him special facilities at Pollsmoor and at Verster prisons and allowed him to almost run an office where the warder and his son did the cooking, served the meal and gave him a telephone.

Christo Brand was Mandela's warder for many years, first on Robben Island and then at Pollsmoor Prison. He has described Mandela's prison life, from the garden and music he loved to how his letters were censored and how he helped hide Mandela's newborn grandchild so he could see and hold him in prison.

A short chapter in Mandela's memoirs, *'The Most Important Person in Any Prisoners Life'* talks about his relationship with warders and how his fellow prisoners devised ways to evade them and communicate with each other. "I always tried to be decent to the warders in my section; hostility was self-defeating. There was no point in having a permanent enemy among the warders. It was ANC's policy to try to educate all people, even our enemies: we believed that all men, even prison service warders, were capable of change, and we did our utmost to try to sway them...Having sympathetic warders facilitated one of our most vital tasks on Robben Island—communication, which was accomplished in two ways; through prisoners whose sentences were completed and were leaving the island, and through contact with visitors. Sometimes letters were sent through visiting lawyers since they were never searched."

While in prison, Mandela studied through the external program of the University of London for a law degree.

There was a plot to rescue Mandela from prison in 1969 by the South African intelligence, which is described by agent Gorden Brown in his memoir, 'Inside Boss'. The intention was to shoot Mandela and show it as an encounter. The plot was foiled by British Intelligence.

In March 1982, Mandela was transferred from Robben Island to Pollsmoor Prison along with other senior ANC leaders. This was to check the growing influence of these leaders on the young generation of black activists imprisoned on Robben Island.

In February 1985, Mandela was offered his freedom by President Botha on the condition that he 'unconditionally rejected violence as a political weapon'. Mandela spurned the offer, making a statement through his daughter Zindzi, "What freedom am I being offered while the organization of the people remains banned? Only free men can negotiate. A prisoner cannot enter into contracts."

Mandela was later moved to Victor Verster Prison and continued to be there until his release. Here, friends and relatives were allowed to visit him. His defense lawyer and long time friend also visited him around this time. He later became Mandela's ambassador to Washington during his presidency.

International pressure continued to mount on the apartheid regime for the release of Nelson Mandela. Mandela was visited several times by the delegates of the Red Cross while in prison. He responded by saying, "To me personally and those who shared the experience of being political prisoners, the Red Cross was a beacon of humanity within the dark inhumane world of political imprisonment." Finally, when De Klerk took over from Botha that Mandela was released in 1990. The event was broadcast live all over the world. The ban on ANC and other anti-apartheid organizations was lifted.

On the day of his release, Mandela gave a speech committing himself to peace and reconciliation with the country's white minority, adding that the ANC's armed struggle would continue. He said, "Our resort to the armed struggle in 1960 with the formation of the military wing of the ANC (Umkhonto we Sizwe) was a purely defensive action against the violence of apartheid. The factors which necessitated the armed struggle still exist today. We have no option but to continue. We express the hope that a climate conducive to a negotiated settlement would be created soon, so that there may no longer be the need for the armed struggle."

Chapter 14
The Victory

Several protests had erupted against the system of apartheid in the 1980's. Suffering for almost forty years, black South Africans took to the streets of various townships across the

Mandela casting his vote for the first time in 1994

country. The protests were chaotic and sporadic and many deaths were reported as the regime responded with violence. In June 1986, the South African government declared a second state of emergency to repress the mass movement that had succeeded in nearly paralyzing the regime. The continuing stand-off between the black majority and the government impelled the new prime minister, De Klerk to lift the ban on political organizations and free Mandela. South Africa's first truly democratic elections in 1994 elected Mandela to the nation's presidency.

It was in 1990 that Mandela declared, "Our march to freedom is irreversible and we must not allow fear to stand in our way." He said, "The majority of South Africans, black and white, recognize that apartheid has no future. It has to be ended by our own decisive mass action in order to build peace and security...there must be an end to white monopoly on political power and a fundamental restructuring of our political and economic systems to ensure that the inequalities of apartheid are addressed and our society thoroughly democratized."

Mandela announced the victory of the ANC in 1994 elections in Johannesburg and addressed the gathering, "My fellow South Africans—the people of South Africa: This is indeed a joyous night. Although not yet final, we have received the provisional results of the election, and are delighted by the overwhelming support for the African National Congress. To all those in the African National Congress and the democratic movement who worked so hard these last few days and through these many decades, I thank you and honor you. To the people of South Africa and the world who are watching—this is a joyous night for the human spirit. This is your victory too. You helped end apartheid; you stood with us through the transition... Tomorrow, the entire ANC leadership and I will be back at our  desks. We are rolling up our sleeves to begin tackling the problems our country faces. We ask you all to join us — go back to your jobs in the morning. Let's get South Africa working. For we must, together and without delay, begin to build a better life for all South Africans. This means creating jobs, building houses, providing education and bringing peace and security for all... The calm and tolerant atmosphere that prevailed during the elections depicts the type of South Africa we can build. It set the tone for the future. We might have our differences, but we are one people with a common destiny in our rich variety of culture, race and tradition... Now is the time for celebration, for South Africans to join together to celebrate the birth of democracy. I raise a glass to you all for working so hard to achieve what can only be called a small miracle."

Delivering his inaugural speech in Cape Town in 1994, Mandela said, "Today we are entering a new era for our country and its people. Today we celebrate not the victory of a party but a victory for all the people of South Africa... Perhaps it was history that ordained that it be here, at the Cape of Good Hope that we should lay the foundation stone of our new nation. For it was here at this Cape, over three centuries ago that there began the fateful convergence of the people of Africa, Europe and Asia on these shores...Ours has been a quest for a constitution freely adopted by the people of South Africa reflecting their wishes and their aspirations. The struggle for democracy has never been a matter pursued by one race, class, religious community or gender among South Africans...Democracy is based on the majority principle. This is especially true in a country such as ours where the vast majorities have been systematically denied their rights. At the same time, democracy also requires that the rights of political and other minorities be safeguarded. In the political order we have established, there will be regular, open and free elections, at all levels of government —central, provincial and municipal. There shall also be a social order which respects completely the culture, language and religious rights of all sections of our society and the fundamental rights of the individual...The task at hand on will not be easy. But you have mandated us to change South Africa from a country in which the majority lived with little hope, to one in which they can live and work with dignity, with a sense of self-esteem and confidence in the future."

"The time for the healing of the wounds has come. The moment to bridge the chasms that divide us has come. The time to build is upon us...We have triumphed in the effort to implant hope in the breasts of the millions of our people. We enter into a covenant that we shall build the society in which all South Africans, both black and white, will be able to walk tall, without any fear in their hearts, assured of their inalienable right to human dignity—a rainbow nation at peace with itself and the world...We must therefore act together as united people, for national reconciliation, for nation building, for the birth of a new world. Let there be justice for all. Let there be peace for all...Never, never and never again shall it be that this beautiful land will again experience the oppression of one by another and suffer the indignity of being the skunk of the world. Let freedom reign! The sun shall never set on so glorious a human achievement! God bless Africa!"

According to Mandela, it was internationalism that facilitated and contributed to the victory. Addressing Cuba's Solidarity Conference which took place in Johannesburg in October 1995, Mandela recalled his trip to Cuba and driving through the streets with Fidal Castro. "He waved and responded to the cheering crowd. Fidel was very humble and only smiled. When we reached the square, I realized that these cheers were not meant for me, they were meant for Fidel Castro." Fidel Castro was one of the first heads of state who was asked to pay a visit to free South Africa. Mandela expressed his deep gratitude to the Cuban people for the selfless contribution made by them to the anti-colonial and anti-apartheid movement in South Africa and conveyed friendship, admiration, respect and concern to the people of Cuba. Hundreds of Cubans had laid down their lives in a struggle that was not theirs and 'the people of South Africa can never ever forget this unparalleled example of selfless internationalism'.

Responding to the pressure being exercised by many powerful countries on South Africa to condemn the suppression of human rights in Cuba, Mandela said that they need to be reminded of their short memory. When the people of South Africa were battling against apartheid, the same countries were supporting the apartheid regime and the war was successfully fought with the support of Cuba and other progressive countries. *"Let me assure you that the African National Congress and the great majority of South Africans will never forget those who stood by us in the darkest years of our struggle against apartheid. Along with the majority of humanity, we are determined to be active participants in the noble effort for a just world order."*

Chapter 15
Negotiating Peace

Nelson Mandela's life symbolizes the triumph of the human spirit. He is one of the few statesmen to have achieved universal respect around the world and across the political gamut. His role in fighting apartheid and being able to steer South Africa through the crisis of its rebirth proved that he is a benevolent negotiator and a peacemaker. Mandela managed to inspire confidence and unite warring political factions. Some people describe his presence as 'near-omnipotent' at the negotiating table with his moral authority and gentle but firm sense of fairness. Nelson Mandela stuck to his commitment to democracy, equality and learning and never answered racism with racism.

The era of apartheid formally came to an end in 1994 but it was evident long before that ANC was going to charter the future of South Africa. Speaking to a free nation, Mandela said, "Friends, Comrades and fellow South Africans. I greet you all in the name of peace, democracy and freedom for all. I stand here before you not as a prophet but as a humble servant of you, the people. Your tireless and heroic sacrifices have made it possible for me to be here today. I therefore place the remaining years of my life in your hands...A man who takes away another man's freedom is a prisoner of hatred, is locked behind the bars of prejudice and narrow-mindedness. I am not truly free if I am taking away someone else's freedom, just as surely as I am not free when my freedom is taken from me. The oppressed and the oppressor alike are robbed of their humanity."

The end of apartheid was the result of a series of negotiations from 1990 to 1993, between the governing National Party, the African National Congress and a wide variety of other political organizations against a backdrop of political violence. In 1974, Harry Schwarz, the Transvaal leader of the United Party along with Mangosuthu Buthelezi signed a five-point plan for racial peace in South Africa which came to be known as Mahlabatini Declaration of Faith. It contained a blueprint for the government of South Africa by consent, opportunity for all, maintenance of racial peace and a Bill of Rights. The decision was taken to adhere to non-violent means of protest.

The first round of meetings between the South African Government and Nelson Mandela were secret in nature and driven by the National Intelligence Service. The first concrete move came during the Botha regime, marking a new phase of the talks. A significant move towards formal negotiations was the unbanning of the ANC by President De Klerk and the release of Nelson Mandela after more than two decades in prison.

Formal negotiations began with a meeting between the African National Congress and the South African government in 1990 at the presidential palace resulting in the *Groote*

Schuur Minute. The two parties committed themselves to resolve the existing climate of violence, indemnity from prosecution for returning exiles and release of political prisoners. In the same year, several new dimensions were added like suspension of the armed struggle by the ANC and its military wing which was called the *Pretoria Minute*. Negotiations took a critical turn with the signing of the *National Peace Accord* in September 1991, by the representatives of twenty seven political organizations, thus paving the path for CODESA (The Convention for a Democratic South Africa) negotiations which was represented by nineteen groups including the South African government. The right wing white Conservative Party and the left wing Pan-Africanist Congress boycotted CODESA. In the period between CODESA I and CODESA II (1991-92), the National Party lost three by-elections to the Conservative Party. A 'whites only' referendum was announced by De Klerk on the issue of reforms and negotiations with 68 per cent of the population voting for it. In June 1992, Boipatong massacre took place, killing many people as a result of which Mandela withdrew his party from the negotiations leading to a breakdown of the CODESA II talks. The ANC also took to the streets with an agenda of 'rolling mass action'. A new urgency was created to the search for a political settlement. In September 1992, the apartheid regime and the ANC agreed on a *Record of Understanding* dealing with a constitutional assembly, an interim government, political prisoners and mass action, resuming the negotiation process.

The assassination of Chris Hani, leader of the SACP and a senior ANC leader in April 1993 by the white right-wingers again brought the country to the brink of disaster but ultimately proved to be a turning point by leading the shift of power in favor of the ANC. The elections were finally held in 1994. ANC won 62 per cent of the votes; Mandela became the president with De Klerk and Thabo Mbeki as deputies. The National party joined the ANC in forming a government of National Unity with 20 per cent votes. Transition continued even after the election till a new constitution was finally adopted in 1995 and the Truth and Reconciliation Commission came into operation and effectively started dealing with politically motivated crimes and atrocities committed during the apartheid era.

Chapter 16
The Leader

Nelson Mandela, after his release from prison in 1990, plunged himself whole heartedly in fulfilling his life's ambition and the goals he and others had set for a free South Africa. South Africa's first multi-racial elections were held in 1994 in which ANC got the majority votes and Mandela

was inaugurated as the President. As President from May 1994 until June 1999, he led the transition to democracy and advocated national and international reconciliation, a contribution recognized and appreciated worldwide. A major step in the reconciliation of blacks and whites was the hosting of 1995 Rugby World Cup and South African team being led to victory by an African. Mandela believed that "South Africa is the most beautiful place on earth…when you combine the natural beauty with the friendliness and cultural diversity of the people."

Combating poverty and deprivation affecting the majority of population was a gigantic task. Mandela initiated the idea of a bread that would feed 5.5 million hungry children in his country. Standing by his promise that 'each child would have something to eat during his presidency', Mandela created a sandwich (bread and peanut butter) which became a major component of a program for poverty stricken rural areas.

Working tirelessly for over eighty years, Former South African President, Nelson Mandela is a great moral and political force, demonstrating all the qualities that make a good leader. He is endowed with a strong and clear vision, and effectively communicates the goal to his people. It was not revenge that he was seeking, insisting that bitterness of the past must be forgotten and the country must take the path of reconciliation with white South Africans. Creation of a new nation where race and color did not matter, a rainbow nation has been his dream. Popularly linked and identified with the freedom movement of South Africa, Mandela's charter extended to the Universal Declaration of Human Rights. "The values of happiness, justice, human dignity, peace and prosperity have a universal application because each and every individual is entitled to them," he said in one of his speeches. "Similarly, no person can truly say it is blessed with happiness, peace and prosperity where others, as human as itself, continue to be afflicted with misery, armed conflict and terrorism and deprivation." Nelson Mandela, time and again has proved to be true to his word and worked with remarkable integrity and consistency.

While he was the president of the country, he believed in delegating authority as opposed to absolute power. Mandela continued to enjoy the reputation of the modest man of the people, someone whom the people continued to relate with. With great calm and poise, he performed all his responsibilities as a fighter, a negotiator and an administrator.

Past half century has witnessed Mandela's image towering over not just South Africa but the world. From an inspirational freedom fighter, through the dark years in prison, to his emergence as the president of a multi-party democracy—the story is awe inspiring. The patient prisoner on Robben Island, smashing stones in a quarry, waiting and watching his people endure decades of brutality–and then a ray of hope as the curtain fell on apartheid and Mandela walked a free man.

A leader is discussed in terms of what he does, but there is something that Mandela did not do and it made history. He declined to run for the second term as president, did not hide his errors and did not stop learning.

Chapter 17
Deepest Fear

Life is a great teacher and time, the greatest healer. Nelson Mandela, all along made an attempt to understand life and create new dimensions for the individual as well as society. He had firm faith in God and displayed understanding across cultural and racial divides. For Mandela, the light of God's path brought forth inner peace and motivation to achieve the objectives. There is no place in his life for unfounded fears. It is liberation from these fears and taking upon ourselves the responsibility to help others grow and flourish that will eventually determine the extent of power that an individual wields.

Our greatest fear is not that we are inadequate, but that we are powerful beyond measure.

It is our light, not our darkness, that frightens us. We ask ourselves, Who am I to be brilliant, gorgeous, handsome, talented and fabulous? Actually, who are you not to be?

You are a child of God. Your playing small does not serve the world. There is nothing enlightened about shrinking so that other people won't feel insecure around you.

We were born to make manifest the glory of God within us. It is not just in some; it is in everyone.

And, as we let our own light shine, we consciously give other people permission to do the same. As we are liberated from our fear, our presence automatically liberates others.

The above speech by Nelson Mandela came out of wide reading, deep thought and understanding of human nature. He calls for sensitivity, compassion and correct perception of the roles that people play in their lives. For some, the greatest fear is that we are too powerful and not as inadequate as we appear to be. For the majority this emerges as a contradiction because most of us believe that we are actually helpless and of no consequence in the larger scheme of things. It is this negativity that is self-destructive. The light Mandela speaks of comes from within and love, compassion and understanding will finally lead us towards growth and understanding of ourselves and those around us. Life without hope is darkness—darkness is fear and leads to self-destruction and absence of all human virtues. We are a combination of divine spark and growth of character which is shaped by the process of socialization. Growth of character is indicated by happiness, peace and sense of fulfillment. Nothing is impossible for a man to achieve provided he walks in harmony with his soul, appreciating the value of integrity and honesty of purpose.

The quote 'Deepest Fear' used by Mandela in his inaugural speech is widely misattributed to Mandela. The actual author is Marianne Willaimson and her book published in 1992 *'Return to Love'* carries these lines.

Chapter 18
The Controversies

A leader and a celebrity—Mandela's life has not been devoid of controversies. A trusted friend of his who also happened to be his personal attorney for over thirty years, Ismail Ayob, was asked at one point of time by Mandela to stop selling material bearing Mandela's signature and account for the proceeds of those that have already been sold. The resultant dispute led Mandela to file an application in the High Court of South Africa. Ayob denied any wrong doing and said that he was a victim of a smear campaign orchestrated by Mandela's advisors. The dispute was widely covered by the media and popularly came to be known as the Ismail Ayob controversy. Ayob was portrayed in bad light and calls were given to ostracize him and his family. The dispute again hit the headlines when Ayob promised to pay R700,000 to Mandela. Some people also sympathized with Ayob saying that he was pitched against a man with iconic status and it is almost impossible for him to prove his point.

Ayob, to begin with was one of the trustees of the Nelson Mandela Trust set up to manage millions of rands of donations coming to Nelson Mandela from prominent people across the world including the Oppenheimer family. It was after Ayob's resignation from the trust in 2006 that the other trustees launched a campaign against him for disbursing the trust money without their consent. Ayob claimed that this money was paid to the South African Revenue Service, to Mandela's children and grandchildren, to Mandela himself, and to an accounting company for four years of accounting work. He was also made to apologize for making defamatory remarks against Mandela in his affidavit.

Nelson Mandela was often criticized for making positive comments about the diamond industry which were interpreted as encouragement extended to the suppliers of blood diamonds. Writing to Edward Zwick, the director of the motion picture *Blood Diamond,* Mandela observed, "...it would be deeply regrettable if the making of the film inadvertently obscured the truth, and, as a result, led the world to believe that an appropriate response might be to cease buying mined diamonds from Africa. ... We hope that the desire to tell a gripping and important real life historical story will not result in the destabilization of African diamond producing countries, and ultimately their peoples."

Media reports attributed these kinds of statements to Mandela's friendship with Harry Oppenheimer, former chairman of De Beers and were also motivated by 'narrow national interests' of South Africa which happens to be a major diamond producer.

Blood Diamond controversy has been kept alive by the ongoing trial of former Liberian president, Charles Taylor at the International Court of Criminal Justice, The Hague.

The former presidential spokesman has described Taylor as 'a man betrayed' and the whole episode as 'the betrayal of the century'. In a statement entitled, 'Charles Taylor, Naomi Campbell, Blood Diamonds and A Man Betrayed,' chief Fani-Kayode said the agreement with Taylor that nothing would be done to him was put in place before President Johnson was elected. "Ironically, the real traitor was not Obasanjo but rather President Sirleaf Johnson of Liberia." The deal with Taylor was that he would agree to step down as president of Liberia and would be given a 'safe haven' in Nigeria. He was escorted to Nigeria which was to be his home for the rest of his life. He was expected to stay out of Liberian politics and not interfere at all with the events there. It was a deal with Taylor that led to a free and fair election in Liberia bringing Johnson to power.

The new focus of the case has been whether Taylor actually gave diamonds to Naomi Campbell, thirteen years ago in South Africa. Taylor has denied ever carrying or trading diamonds. The prosecution called actress Mia Farrow in the Sierra Leone Court in connection with the case against Taylor on 9 August, 2010 following supermodel Naomi Campbell's testimony on the fifth. The issue is that Naomi Campbell received a blood diamond from Taylor. Naomi admitted briefly meeting Taylor during a visit to Nelson Mandela's home in South Africa but added that she did not know who he was. She has time and again insisted that she did not want to be involved in the case in any manner whatsoever. Naomi, in fact assaulted a cameraman during an interview with ABC News television when she was questioned over the diamond issue.

Campbell finally testified that she did receive 'two or three' stones in the middle of the night from two unidentified men after a dinner with Taylor, Nelson Mandela and others. She denied giving false testimony at the war crimes trial, saying she had 'nothing to gain'. Her former agent, Carole White and Mia Farrow had told the two judges that Campbell had accepted the gifts and also boasted about it the next day. Both testified that the pouch of stones was given next day to the then director of the Nelson Mandela Children's Fund, Jeremy Ractliffe who handed them over to the police. The South African police are still trying to find out what happened to those stones.

Meanwhile, Zimbabwe opened the first sale of diamonds from the Marange fields after a partial lifting of ban by the international regulators. The ban was imposed after the military violently took control of the mines. Around 9,00,000 carats were on sale, according to Abbey Chikane, the monitor from the international Kimberley Process which is charged with preventing trade in 'blood diamonds'. Kimberly had blocked the sales from Marange over abuses by the military and 'horrific and unacceptable violence against civilians'.*

More recently, painting of a dead Nelson Mandela sparked off a controversy. The painting which showed Mandela dead, scantily clothed, undergoing an autopsy sparked off unrest in Cape Town. The mural is on display in Johannesburg's Hyde Park shopping mall showing Mandela's body surrounded by Archbishop Desmond Tutu, former presidents FW de Klerk and Thabo Mbeki, and politicians Trevor Manuel and Helen Zille, all wearing seventeenth century costumes. South

---
Times of India, 8 December, 2010

Africa's youngest AIDS activist, twelve year old Nkosi Johnson who died in 2001, uses a scalpel to tear into the icon's lifeless body.

South African artist Yuill Damaso's controversial painting that depicts a dead Nelson Mandela undergoing an autopsy with various South African politicians looking on

The work is based on a seventeenth century Rembrandt masterpiece called 'The Anatomy Lesson of Dr Nicholas Tulp'. Some say that it is meant to be a tribute to Mandela. "Nelson Mandela is a great man, but he's just a man," Damaso told the BBC. "The eventual passing of Mr Mandela is something that we will have to face, as individuals, as a nation."

What Damaso chose as a subject is taboo in South African culture. Showing a live man dead is associated with witchcraft. The ANC issued a statement saying, "It is in bad taste, disrespectful, and it is an insult and affront to values of our society... In African society it is a foreign act of ubuthakathi (witchcraft) to kill a living person... This so-called work of art... is also racist. It goes further by violating (Mandela's) dignity by stripping him naked in the glare of curious onlookers". The ANC also criticized the South African Mail and Guardian newspaper for running a front-page photo Friday of the unfinished painting, describing it as 'gutter journalism and soul-less sensationalism.'

The artist incidentally received a phone call from a friend of one of Mandela's daughters telling him how the painting had upset her as she was linking it to a recent death in the family. Mandela's thirteen year old granddaughter had died in a car accident on her way home from a concert on the eve of the World Cup's opening. The tragedy impelled Mandela to cancel his appearance at the World Cup's opening ceremony. Mandela has been credited with bringing the World Cup to South Africa, the first time the world's largest sporting event has ever been played on African soil. Despite criticism and opposition, the Hyde Park mall has decided to keep the painting in place in line with the freedom of expression espoused by the country's constitution.

As Nelson Mandela celebrated his ninety second birthday, the world is witnessing the battle for his legacy worth millions of dollars intensify. There are reports of bitter feuds between his friends and relatives over the control of his name. The disputes are at the level of his family from his three marriages, the ANC and the various foundations and charities he had set up after his retirement. Fred Khumalo,

South African author and columnist terms all this as nasty. "People are fighting while he is still alive."

Nelson Mandela celebrated his ninety second birthday

Mandla Mandela, Nelson Mandela's grandson said, "As a family, we are united in that the legacy of Madiba belongs to his family first and to the ANC." Mandla has been recently initiated into national politics with his getting elected to the parliament in the last election. His influence also stems from the fact that he is the newly appointed traditional chief of Nelson Mandela's birthplace, the village of Mvezo. Mandla once said, "In my veins runs the blood of the Mandela's which has been around for centuries."

It is alleged that in 2008, Snuki Zikalala, the former head of news at the South African Broadcasting Corporation, told the *Sunday World* Newspaper that Mandla had been paid 3 million rand by the public broadcaster for rights to cover Nelson Mandela's funeral–something which was flatly denied by Mandla.

Nelson Mandela Museum had plans to protect his birthplace as a heritage site. Mandla was involved with them in a bitter feud and accused them of "benefitting and profiting from my grandfather's name...They give nothing to his people...Mandela's people are dying here (in Mvezo) from AIDS, yet 46664 (a campaign for AIDS) have done nothing here".* Mandla is only one of the few Mandela's claiming the legacy of the icon.

Another controversy surrounded Mandela's appearance at the football World cup. The ANC government's sports minister and Mandela's grandson gave contradictory speeches in the build up to the event while claiming to speak on behalf of the former president. The minister said Mandela wanted to attend the ceremony while his grandson confirmed that he preferred to be at home.

Mandela's World Cup appearance

Mandela graced the closing ceremony of World Cup football along with his wife, Graca Machel who helped a frail Mandela to raise his hand and wave at the crowd.

*Interview with South Africa's Mail and *Guardian* newspaper.

It is righty anticipated that the battles over his legacy between his family, associates and political comrades is sure to take a nasty turn on his demise. May be, in future we will be witnessing history repeating itself –the family of Martin Luther King Jr., globally recognized black civil rights activist, is still fighting for his estate, forty years after his death.

Mandela is reported to have called a family meeting to discuss his will which essentially gives a large portion of his estate to the Nelson Mandela Foundation and remaining to his children, his grandson Mandla and his current wife, Graca Machel. The media reports said that the meeting was not conclusive, an indication of the weakening grip of Mandela over his personal affairs.

Chapter 19
The Nobel Peace Prize

The Nobel Prize in Peace 1993 was awarded jointly to Nelson Mandela and Frederik Willem de Klerk *'for their work for the peaceful termination of the apartheid regime, and for laying the foundations for a new democratic South Africa'.*

Nelson Mandela

De Klerk

In his acceptance speech and Nobel lecture, Nelson Mandela thanked the Norwegian Nobel Committee for having conferred the highest honor upon him and gave credit to Archbishop Desmond Tutu for his contribution to the peaceful struggle against apartheid who was also awarded the Nobel Peace Prize. Mandela did not forget to add Martin Luther King Jr.'s name and highlighted his great contribution to the civil rights movement in the US. He said, "We speak here of the challenge of the dichotomies of war and peace, violence and non-violence, racism and human dignity, oppression and repression, liberty, human rights, poverty and freedom from want...We stand here today as nothing more than a representative of the millions of our people who dared to rise up against a social system whose very essence is war, violence, racism, oppression, repression and the impoverishment of an entire people...I am also here today as a representative of the millions of people across the globe, the anti-apartheid movement, the governments and organizations that joined with us, not to fight against South Africa as a country or any of its people, but to oppose an inhuman system and sue for a speedy end to the apartheid crime against humanity...These countless human beings, both inside and outside our country, had the nobility of spirit to stand in the path of tyranny and injustice, without seeking selfish gain. They recognized that an injury to one is an injury to all and therefore acted together in defense of justice and a common human decency...Because of their courage and persistence for many years, we can, today, even set the dates when all humanity will join together to celebrate one of the outstanding human victories of our century."

Mandela stressed upon the sacrifices that have been made to reach the destination by millions of South Africans. These are the people who suffered for 'liberty, peace, human dignity and fulfillment'. "In front of this distinguished audience, we commit the new South Africa to the relentless pursuit of the purposes defined in the World Declaration on the Survival, Protection and Development of Children...The reward of which we have spoken will and must also be measured by the happiness and welfare of the mothers and fathers of these children, who must walk the earth without fear of being robbed, killed for political or material profit, or spat upon because they are beggars...They too must be relieved of the heavy burden of despair which they carry in their hearts, born of hunger, homelessness and unemployment...Thus shall we live, because we will have created a society which recognizes that all people are born equal, with each entitled in equal measure to life, liberty, prosperity, human rights and good governance...Such a society should never allow again that there should be prisoners of conscience nor that any person's human right should be violated...Neither should it ever happen that once more the avenues to peaceful change are blocked by usurpers who seek to take power away from the people, in pursuit of their own, ignoble purposes."

Mandela, on this occasion appealed to the military rulers in Burma to release Aung San Suu Kyi and enter into a meaningful dialogue for the sake of the Burmese people. He complimented De Klerk for his courage to admit that a terrible wrong had been done to South Africa.

"We live with the hope that as she battles to remake herself, South Africa, will be like a microcosm of the new world that is striving to be born...This must be a world of democracy and respect for human rights, a world freed from the horrors of poverty, hunger, deprivation and ignorance, relieved of the threat and the scourge of civil wars and external aggression and unburdened of the great tragedy of millions forced to become refugees...The processes in which South Africa and southern Africa as a whole are engaged, beckon and urge us all that we take this tide at the flood and make of this region a living example of what all people of conscience would like the world to be...We do not believe that this Nobel Peace Prize is intended as a commendation for matters that have happened and passed...We hear the voices which say that it is an appeal from all those, throughout the universe, who sought an end to the system of apartheid...We understand their call, that we devote what remains of our lives to the use of our country's unique and painful experience to demonstrate, in practice, that the normal condition for human existence is democracy, justice, peace, non-racism, non-sexism, prosperity for everybody, a healthy environment and equality and solidarity among the peoples...Moved by that appeal and inspired by the eminence you have thrust upon us, we undertake that we too will do what we can to contribute to the renewal of our world so that none should, in future, be described as the 'wretched of the earth'...Let it never be said by future generations that indifference, cynicism or selfishness made us fail to live up to the ideals of humanism which the Nobel Peace Prize encapsulates...Let the strivings of us all, prove Martin Luther King Jr. to have been correct, when he said that humanity can no longer be tragically bound to the starless midnight of racism and war...Let the efforts of us all, prove that he was not a mere dreamer when he spoke of the beauty of genuine brotherhood and peace being more precious than diamonds or silver or gold...*Let a new age dawn!*"

Chapter 20
Accolades and Honors

"For to be free is not merely to cast off one's chains, but to live in a way that respects and enhances the freedom of others."—Nelson Mandela

The statue of Mandela in Parliament Square, London

Not many would doubt the political achievements of Nelson Mandela for which he was awarded the Nobel Prize and many more recognitions. He has received more than 250 awards including honorary degrees. Mandela indeed is a great man with wonderful sense of humor, honesty and humility. There is a statue of his in Johannesburg and another in Parliament Square in London.

Many streets and bridges across the world are named after him and postage stamps released.

Nelson Mandela bridge in Johannesburg

The Nelson Mandela Stadium in Port Elizabeth, South Africa, built for 2010 FIFA World Cup has a capacity of 46,500 spectators.

On 14 April, 2010, Mandela was honored for his contribution to dismantling apartheid by Africa Peace Award

(ABETO). ABETO is a non-profit organization dedicated to peaceful conflict resolution, peaceful co-existence, tolerance, democracy and good governance across Africa.

Mr Mandela was selected as the first recipient of this prestigious award for his life-long commitment to peace, justice and equality. ABETO Chairman Moses Musana said, "We are here today to acknowledge, recognize and thank Nelson Mandela for the selfless contributions he made to liberate South Africa from the apartheid regime."

Fighter for liberation of South Africa Nelson Mandela on a 1988 USSR commemorative stamp

ABETO Chairman, Moses Musana presents the ABETO Africa Peace Award to Achmat Dangor, Nelson Mandela Foundation, CEO

Achmat Dangor, Nelson Mandela Foundation, CEO said, "The Nelson Mandela Foundation Centre for Memory and Dialogue welcomes the honor bestowed on its founder Mr Nelson Mandela and we will ensure the award occupies a special place in the Centre of Memory and Dialogue."

The United Nations General Assembly has declared July 18, Nelson Mandela International Day in recognition of the South African anti-apartheid leader's contribution to peace. A resolution was unanimously adopted by the 192 member world body calling for commemorating 18 July, Mandela's birthday starting from 2010. His ninety second birthday was celebrated worldwide with community service and pledging to his ideals of equality, forgiveness and humanity.

Mandela was awarded the Arthur Ashe Courage Award at the 2009 ESPY, an award presented annually to people whose contributions transcend sports. The award was accepted by his daughter, Zindzi Mandela and grandson, Zondwa Mandela on his behalf. Mandela's unforgettable moment was when he donned a Springbok rugby shirt and cap for the 1995 Rugby World Cup, presenting the William Webb Ellis Cup to Springbok captain Francois Pienaar, delighting sports fans across South Africa.

Former presidents Nelson Mandela, FW de Klerk and Archbishop Desmond Tutu have accepted honorary membership of Die Suid-Afrikaanse Akademie vir Wetenskap en Kuns. The academy said that De Klerk was given the honor for his courage in laying the foundation for a post-apartheid South Africa and Mandela for reconciling different population groups. It lauded Tutu for encouraging forgiveness as chairperson of the Truth and Reconciliation Commission.

According to an article in *Newsweek* magazine, 'Mandela rightly occupies an untouched place in the South African imagination. He's the national liberator, the savior, its Washington and Lincoln rolled into one'. Besides the Nobel Peace Prize, Mandela has received the *Order of Merit* from Queen Elizabeth II and the *Presidential Medal of Freedom* from George W Bush. In 2004, the city of Johannesburg bestowed its highest honor on Mandela by granting him the *Freedom of the city* at a ceremony in Orlando, Soweto. He was greeted by 45,000 children in the city of Toronto during his tour of Canada in 1988. Mandela is also a recipient of *Bharat Ratna* from the Indian government and the *Lenin Peace Prize* from the Soviet Union. In 1992, he received *Nishan-e-Pakistan*, the highest civilian award of that country.

Many artists have dedicated their songs to the icon. *The Specials* recorded their popular number, *Free Nelson Mandela in 1983;* followed by *Stevie Wonder's* Oscar winning song *I Just Called To Say I Love You* in 1985. In 1990, Hong Kong rock band *Beyond* released a popular Cantonese song, *'Days of Glory'*. The anti-apartheid song featured lyrics referring to Mandela's heroic struggle for racial equality. The group Ladysmith Black Mambazo accompanied Mandela to the Nobel Peace Prize ceremony in Oslo, Norway in 1993.

The motion picture, *Mandela and De Klerk* told the story of Mandela's release from prison. Another feature film, *Goodbye Bafana* focused on Mandela's life and was screened at the Berlin film festival in February 2007. Many biographies and books have been written on Mandela.

Playing the Enemy: Nelson Mandela and the Game that Made a Nation, a book by *John Carlin,* spotlights the role of the 1995 Rugby World Cup win in post-apartheid South Africa.

Chapter 21
International Affairs

It is difficult to explore Mandela's inner core for he trusts and opens himself only to very few people. A protective friend and a fearsome foe, Nelson Mandela is a man of intense, passionate loves and hates. Superficial appearances fail to impress him and he looks for hidden motives. Enterprising, original and intuitive, his instincts dislike interference and it is impossible to deceive him. Mandela often seems to be

The elders–group of past and present world leaders

withdrawing from the world—these are moments of healing. All his life, he has been identifying with the oppressed, forever willing to help and care for them. He treats others in an agreeable, affectionate and tactful manner and does not hide his affection which has ensured a large circle of friends and a strong community spirit.

Discussing personal attributes of Nelson Mandela is not quite out of place here since they shaped his relations with other countries and world leaders. Nelson Mandela had strongly criticized the NATO intervention in Kosovo in 1999, calling it an attempt by world's powerful nations to police the entire world. A number of Mandela's speeches carried criticisms of the foreign policy of the George Bush administration. He expected the UN to be more in control at the time of Iraq war and make an attempt to prevent US military intervention. He said, "It is a tragedy. What is happening, what Bush is doing. But Bush is now undermining the UN." South Africa would support action against Iraq only if it is ordered by UN. He called upon the US citizens to protest against the Bush administration and also urged the countries with veto powers to oppose this decision in the UN Security Council. "What I am condemning is that one power with a president who has no foresight, who cannot think properly, is now wanting to plunge the world into a holocaust." He added, 'US has a very bad human rights record and highlighted the atrocities committed in the past like dropping atomic bombs on Japan during World War II. Mandela referred to the British Prime Minister Tony Blair as the 'foreign minister of the United States'.

Strong criticism had been leveled against the Jewish South African judge, Richard Goldstone by the Israeli government officials for his decision to send back twenty eight black South Africans to death while serving as a judge during the anti-apartheid years. "The judge who sentenced black people to death ... is a man of double standards," Knesset Speaker Reuven Rivlin proclaimed. "Such a person should not be allowed to lecture a democratic state defending itself against terrorists." Israeli Deputy Foreign Minister, Danny Ayalon insisted, "This so-called respected judge is using this report in order to atone for his sins," likening Goldstone's statement that he was forced to uphold the laws of an unjust regime. Goldstone has been labeled as a man who took an active part in the racist policies of one of the cruelest regimes of the twentieth century.

Goldstone's apartheid era judicial decisions are definitely a blot on his record but his critics often overlook the crucial role he played in steering South Africa through its transition to democracy and ensuring a peaceful shift of power—a role for which Nelson Mandela embraced him and appointed him to South Africa's highest court. In fact, it was Israel who armed the apartheid regime from mid 1970's to the early 1990's, doing far more to aid the apartheid regime. By 1979, South Africa had become the Israeli defense industry's single largest customer, accounting for 35 per cent of military exports and dwarfing other clients such as Argentina, Chile, Singapore and Zaire. The nuclear cooperation involved South Africa supplying yellowcake uranium to Israel while dozens of Israelis came to Pretoria to work on the nuclear missile program at the secret Overberg testing range. Israel was profiting heavily from weapon sales to Pretoria at that time. Not all of the weapons Israel sold were used in external wars, and there is no denying that Israeli arms helped prolong the rule of an immoral and racist regime.

Robert Mugabe, the president of Zimbabwe had been globally condemned for corruption, ineffective administration, political oppression and the fighting which killed 3000 people in the 1980's. There was only one common thread linking Mandela and Mugabe—both were national liberators. Mandela rarely spoke out on Zimbabwe, fuelling the rumors that he is not exercising his influence on Mugabe to moderate his policies. But in 2000, Mandela made a statement referring to Mugabe saying that he is 'one of those leaders who had over stayed their welcome'. In 2007, Mandela tried to persuade Mugabe to relinquish office 'sooner than later' with 'a modicum of dignity'. Mugabe did not pay heed to this advise ultimately leading to a deep crisis at the Zimbabwean presidential election to which Mandela responded by calling it the 'tragic failure of leadership' in the country.

Beginning of the decade 1990 saw South Africa reviving its ties with other countries. Algeria, Bulgaria, Italy, Libya, Mauritania, Mexico, Morocco, the Netherlands, Singapore, Sweden, Thailand and Tunisia announced the end of trade sanctions against South Africa in 1991 and 1992, paving the way for full diplomatic relations. President Mandela's inauguration in May 1994 was attended by representatives of 169 countries and by 1995, South Africa had established diplomatic ties with around 147 countries. The prominent among them were the People's Republic of China which was strongly critical of the apartheid regime. The Republic of China had been an important source of investment, trade and tourism for South Africa. Taipei made substantial contributions to South Africa's reconstruction and development program and to other areas of development.

In addition to all this, the year 1994 marked a watershed in South Africa's international relations, as it was welcomed into regional and international organizations, such as the UN, the Organization of African Unity (OAU), the Non-aligned Movement and many others. The UN already had played an important role in South Africa's transition to democracy beginning in August 1992, when United Nations Security Council Resolution 772 authorized the United Nations Observer Mission in South Africa (UNOMSA) to help suppress political violence.

The United Nations Security Council lifted the arms embargo known as Security Council Resolution 418, in May 1994. In 1995, UN waved off most of the amount (around US$ 100 million) which Pretoria was supposed to pay in dues and annual payments for the years its UN participation had been suspended. The amount was waved off considering that Pretoria was not obliged to make back payments on behalf of the apartheid regime.

South Africa resumed its seat in the OAU in June 1994. At the summit held in Tunis, Nelson Mandela reiterated his support for other African leaders and South Africa's solidarity with African interests. The same year, South Africa rejoined the British Commonwealth of Nations and also became the eleventh member of the South African Development Community (SADC). SADC had been established in 1979 to make an attempt to reduce regional economic dependence on South Africa. In 1992, the ten member states agreed to reorganize as SADC to strengthen regional ties and to work towards formation of a regional market. Another step forward the same year was South Africa's gaining membership of the South Atlantic

Peace and Cooperation Zone and attending their meeting in Brasilia. A declaration affirming the South Atlantic as a nuclear-weapons-free zone was also signed in addition to agreements on trade and environmental protection in the region.

South Africa had gained a lot after the establishment of multi-racial democracy in terms of universal goodwill. Before Mandela took over the reins of the country, his support to Yaser Arafat, Fidel Castro and Colonel Qaddafi was condemned by the western world. Mandela retorted saying, "What concerns me is the foreign policy of those countries, especially in so far as it relates to us (South Africa). Those countries who are committed to assisting the anti-apartheid forces in our country are our friends."

Mandela's cabinet had also passed a provisional approval of arms sales to Syria, an act which provoked Clinton administration to threaten South Africa with suspension of US aid. It was clear to everyone that good relations were important to both the countries. In a speech in New York City during the summer of 1990, Mandela thanked the American people for taking such an interest in him and his struggle. "You, the people, never abandoned us," he said. "From behind the granite walls, political prisoners could hear loud and clear your voice of solidarity.... We are winning because you made it possible."

Mandela has a record of being a good negotiator and a president. In July 2000, a power sharing agreement between the Tutsi-dominated army and Hutu rebels in Burundi seemed likely and Mandela navigated the negotiations, ending Burundi's seven year old civil war.

Chapter 22
Nelson Mandela and the Media

Mandela has shared a unique relationship with the media with a record of visits to every newspaper editor in South Africa and sometimes even going to the extent of breaking his schedules to visit media headquarters. This image making, as is believed in political circuits has helped Mandela a great deal in dispensing his duties as president, raising funds, and promoting trade and investment.

Mandela is a living example of a leader who has made enormous sacrifices towards an ideal of a racially integrated democracy, keeping the communication channels open with the enemies and finally negotiating them out of power. His commitment to justice, reconciliation and moral integrity has been constantly highlighted by the media. Another aspect of his personality drawing admiration has been the ease with which he interacts with the rich and the powerful. He is not shy in asking for funds. Mandela has a child-like sense of humor and even his enemies admit that he is a wonderful human being.

Conciliatory gestures have been a hallmark of Mandela's leadership. He paid a visit to Verwoerd's widow, the African prime minister who devised apartheid and another visit to Botha, former president who lacked the courage to release Mandela unconditionally. His approach drew the wrath of left-wing blacks who felt that Mandela was too generous  to whites. But a country where the whites still dominated the economy, his approach was necessary and farsighted. Mandela refused to be the 'president for life' unlike many other leaders of the continent, stepping down in 1999. He continued to work behind the scenes but carefully observed the protocol of maintaining public silence on domestic political issues.

John Battersby, who is the editor-in-chief of *The Sunday Independent,* a national sunday newspaper based in Johannesburg has been a long time Mandela watcher. He has written about some of his experiences with Mandela which were published as an article in *The Christian Science Monitor.* "As Nelson Mandela prepares to step down after five years as president, South Africans are beginning to reflect on what makes him so special and what it is about him they will truly miss...Mr Mandela, who emerged from twenty seven years in prison to negotiate the end of apartheid with his jailers, leaves a legacy of principled leadership and racial reconciliation...His critics complain that he has tried to quell white apprehensions at the expense of meeting black aspirations. It remains to be seen whether his successors will be able to redress stark racial inequalities without undermining confidence in one of Africa's most robust economies."

Battersby has vivid memories of the day when Mandela walked out of a prison warder's house after nearly three decades in prison. "I'll never forget that moment. It was a hot summer's day and the surrounding vineyards were shimmering under a clear blue sky. Local and international media thronged the entrance of the prison...Time stood still during the hour in which we waited for Mandela...A delegation of anti-apartheid leaders, including Mr Mandela's controversial wife at the time, Winnie, had entered the prison by car and headed down the road to the warder's house... But when the moment arrived and I saw the tall figure of Mandela striding toward the media throng, I lost all sense of time and ego and walked towards him with a broad smile. He noticed me, smiled back and walked up to shake my hand."

"Mandela's unique style of reaching out to whites while stressing the need for black empowerment has been the key to a relatively peaceful transition from apartheid to black majority rule...In balancing these potentially explosive forces, Mandela has laid the foundation for the next stage of the transition–a real transfer of economic power to blacks and a more rapid Africanization of the civil service and other institutions...Mandela's most abiding contribution to South Africa's emerging democracy may be the support he gave to the creation and execution of Archbishop Desmond Tutu's Truth and Reconciliation Commission. He resisted overwhelming pressure from within the ANC to downplay human rights violations committed by exiled ANC cadres who'd been in charge of detention camps outside the country, where ANC dissidents were held...The vital moment came last October when Mandela, as head of state, accepted the Truth Commission report which, while indicting apartheid, also had harsh words for ANC members guilty of gross human rights abuses...South Africans of all races will look back in a generation or two and will be indebted to Mandela for taking this important moral stand. It is a cornerstone of the emerging South African democracy and the only basis on which to build a moral society."

There are times when Mandela speaks about himself with a sense of detachment. Anthony Simpson, the official biographer of Nelson Mandela has described a 'striking personality change between the impulsive and impatient forty-something revolutionary of the late 1950's and the measured and dignified seventy year-old who stepped out of prison in 1990'. The Mandela we see today has made his journey through deprivation, hardship and separation from his loved ones during his years in prison and has evolved into a compassionate and self-disciplined leader.

Reporting on his relationship with Graca Machel and their marriage on his eightieth birthday, the media said that it is the best thing that could have happened to Mandela even though they had to work out compromises. Ms Machel would spend two weeks of every month in Mozambique, where she is a prominent public figure, and two weeks at Mandela's Johannesburg home.

Mandela's popularity grew with the poor and the downtrodden. NEHAWU, a progressive public service union that engages itself in championing the cause of the poor and the working class, came out with a press release on Mandela's ninety second birthday urging the people to adopt his spirit of sacrifice and serve the poor with dignity and respect. "We urge all Africans and the citizens of the world to embrace this day and participate in its activities and contribute to their societies by extending a helping hand and taking care of those who are poor and vulnerable."

Wishing Mandela more health and many more years of happiness and service to the nation, the union called on all its members and South Africans to spend a minimum of sixty seven minutes of their time making a positive contribution in their communities to mark the annual World Mandela Day on 18 July and in celebration of Nelson Mandela's life and legacy–a befitting honor to a legend who never wavered in the face of dangers on the path of seeking justice for the oppressed and the vulnerable.

Mandela's image has been looming large on his successors. South Africans feel highly indebted to him, he occupies a special place in the South African imagination, his successors are expected to emulate him instead of dealing with the challenges which the country now faces. His distinctive style has raised expectations from other leaders. "Fusing shut the national wounds was Mandela's raison d'être, and subsequent South African presidents have been judged by their talent for mimicking him. It's no stretch to say that Mandela's template helped ruin Thabo Mbeki's presidency."

When Mbeki succeeded Mandela in 1999, the priority shifted from healing the country psychologically to the economic programs which were expected to pay rich dividends. Mbeki was in for a rude shock by the media—"Where Mr Mandela projects warmth of spirit and generosity, Mr Mbeki appears manipulative and calculating," South Africa's *Sunday Times* damned him in an editorial. "Where Mr Mandela inspires affection, even love, Mr Mbeki evokes uncertainty and fear."

Zuma stood in contrast to Mbeki's dry, technocratic style. Using Mandela's nickname, Zuma explained, "He made reconciliation the central theme of his term of office. We will not deviate from that nation-building task. Thank you, Madiba, for showing us the way." Zuma acknowledged the fact that he would be judged by the standards set by Mandela. But with passing years, the president-as-healer is not what South Africa needs. What is required is a leader who can address the socio-economic issues.

As Nelson Mandela turned ninety, Newsweek had a look at how an icon helped shape the destiny of a nation. An article titled, 'Madiba Magic' traced the events starting from Mandela's first day out of prison to the contributions that he made thereafter. "In spite of that legendary fist-punching image, Nelson Mandela's first day of freedom was almost a disaster. While the world celebrated his release, Cape Town was in chaos. Drunken looters terrorized the waiting crowd, taking at least two lives—including one man who was kicked and stabbed to death in front of a television crew. When Mandela's handlers finally let him appear—more than four hours late—his lackluster speech disappointed not only for its hesitant delivery but for its tired rhetoric about the need to nationalize South Africa's mines. Within twenty four hours, the market responded: sales by foreign investors wiped the equivalent of about $1 billion off share values on the Johannesburg Stock Exchange. "He didn't necessarily miss the boat," one political commentator said "but he did miss an opportunity for reconciliation." The mistake was not repeated by Mandela. Even though he appeared frail at a London concert to honor his birthday, but as his voice grew stronger and the smile appeared on his face, the magic remained undimmed. "His articulate and reasoned responses were a pitch-perfect mix of informality and sharp analysis." His message of racial inclusion was unambiguous. Mandela said, "Whites are fellow South Africans. We want them to be safe and know we appreciate the contribution they have made to this country." Another remarkable fact was the absence of bitterness about his years in prison. There was a certain calmness about him. When interviewed and asked, "How in the world he was able to be in the same room with white people and not hate them," he replied in the most quiet and humble voice, "If I had allowed myself to become bitter, I would have died in prison."

In another write up, a reporter who had been covering apartheid in South Africa attempted to examine fact and hype in Clint Eastwood's film, *Invictus*. In an ealy scene from *Invictus*, a group of white African men surround Mandela's security detail. By the time the film ends, the white and black guards bond over soccer, rugby and the leader is being kept safe. The title of the film comes from the poem that inspired Mandela in prison. At one level, the film is a blockbuster about South Africa's battle to win the Rugby World Cup in 1995, at the other level, it is a skillful attempt to look at the difference an inspirational leader can make. Mandela realized that his country's re-entry into the world sports arena was a strong blow to the whites. His athletes had deteriorated during the years of isolation. To inspire his team, Mandela wore the Springbok jersy onto the field for the rugby final.

"Even today, as South Africa is struggling against problems like massive HIV infection rates, rampant crime and growing corruption, it's a gesture that black and white alike still remember as a turning point. That makes *Invictus* an appropriate tribute to a man of vision."

Gorden Brown, writing in *Time,* pointed out how age has not weakened Mandela's urge for justice saying, "Nelson Mandela to me is not just the greatest statesman but the greatest man now living, embodying one of the greatest triumphs of human spirit... No prisoner's cell could diminish Mandela; by the time of his release, his courage and magnanimity had become the greatest beacon of hope for men and women in every continent of the world." Graca Machel said, "He symbolizes a much broader forgiveness and understanding and reaching out." Rightly so–if it was otherwise South Africa could have been in flames. Mandela was always more than a man of his times.

Apartheid was just one of the few hurdles that Mandela crossed. There were many more challenges coming his way–his work on HIV/AIDS and launching of a crusade to give education to every child in the world. Mandela is an inspirational leader, demonstrating optimism and belief that no task is unachievable. To many, he is the closest thing to a saint in their lives. It is a shocking fact that Mandela was on the terror list. His fame eclipses those of presidents; he wields moral authority unmatched by any political or religious leader. The adulation refuses to fade. Mandela used and understood the power of a celebrity–something he used effectively against apartheid and also to reach out to a global audience with his vision.

Mandela's contribution goes beyond dismantling apartheid–he was also instrumental in bringing about greatest transformations of the past century–the emergence of nation–states which were previously European colonies. Whenever complimented, he replies with his characteristic modesty, *"I was not a messiah, but an ordinary man who had become a leader because of extraordinary circumstances."*

Chapter 23
Beyond Politics

After his retirement in 1999, Nelson Mandela established the *Nelson Mandela Foundation*. The foundation embodies the spirit of reconciliation, *ubuntu* and social justice. Since 2006, the vision of the foundation has been to propagate Mr Mandela's legacy by contributing to the making of a just society by promoting the vision, values and work of its founder and convening dialogue around critical social issues.

Mandela, throughout his life has had unshakable faith in dialogue and the ability to listen and speak to others. The Foundation provides a non-partisan platform to address critical social issues. There are four guiding principles behind the five year Strategic Plan of the foundation starting with memory and dialogue work through its centre of Memory and Dialogue. Even after retirement, Nelson Mandela continues to be actively involved in managing the Founder's Office, which is top priority for the Foundation. In order to complete existing projects and fulfill future commitments, necessary partners will be found. The work of the Nelson Mandela

Foundation must be aligned explicitly and unambiguously with that of its two sister charity organizations—the Nelson Mandela Children's Fund and the Mandela Rhodes Foundation.

The main activity undertaken by the Nelson Mandela Memory Program is that of maintaining the memory resources on the life and times of its founder which are scattered geographically and across a range of legal and other jurisdictions. The objective is an integrated information resource on the life and times of Mandela. Besides locating and documenting, the department also has the responsibility of promoting and making information accessible. The

Entrance to the Nelson Mandela Foundation office

reliability of the resources are judged through research and analysis involving verification of memory resources in dialogue with scholars and historical participants, interrogation of texts, contexts and narratives and integrated research services.

The dialogue program aims to develop and sustain a platform promoting Mandela's legacy. The Foundation utilizes the history, experience, values, vision and leadership of its founder to enable discourses on important social issues thereby contributing to policy decision-making.

South Africa has emerged out of deeply rooted racial, cultural and political divides and continues to face a range of complex challenges. The Foundation strives to maintain the original spirit of inclusive and open dialogue that broke the political deadlock in South Africa. It intends to bring about meaningful dialogue among all relevant stakeholders. The Memory Program will promote the use of resources by audiences all over the world with special access to systemically disadvantaged communities.

The Foundation is committed to providing Mandela with a full and integrated personal office as long as he lives. Although his public engagements have been on the decline, requests keep pouring in.

Since his retirement, one of Mandela's primary commitments has been to fight against AIDS. He supports 46664 AIDS fund raising campaign, named after his prison number. 46664 is a South African-based, independent, not-for-profit entity wholly owned by the Nelson Mandela

Foundation. Mandela speaks at various international forums espousing the cause and generating awareness ever since his son died of AIDS in January, 2000. Stephanie Nolen has chronicled Mandela's AIDS activism in the book 28: Stories of AIDS in Africa. Nelson Mandela's campaign to help raise global awareness of AIDS/HIV, 46664 aims to highlight the emergency of AIDS/HIV through unique live events and music related initiatives.

The 46664 campaign is an initiative to inspire individual and collective action towards an AIDS-free world. At its core, the campaign is about bringing hope and inspiration to all affected by HIV/AIDS. Thus 46664 raises awareness about the HIV/AIDS pandemic and the underlying issues that influence it, such as poverty, lack of education, gender inequality, lack of access to health facilities and the denial of economic opportunities.

These objectives are achieved through campaigns in Africa as well as other countries through staging of concerts, sporting events and fund raisers. It draws upon global network of ambassadors and celebrities to educate, empower and engage those who are infected and affected by the disease and raise awareness among the younger generation. 46664, Mandela's prison number and the slogan 'It's in our hands' given by him became the icon for promoting a global HIV/AIDS awareness campaign.

Speaking at the first 46664 concert held at Greenpoint Stadium in Cape Town in 2003, Nelson Mandela pointed out, *'AIDS is no longer just a disease, it is a human rights issue. The more we lack the courage and the will to act, the*

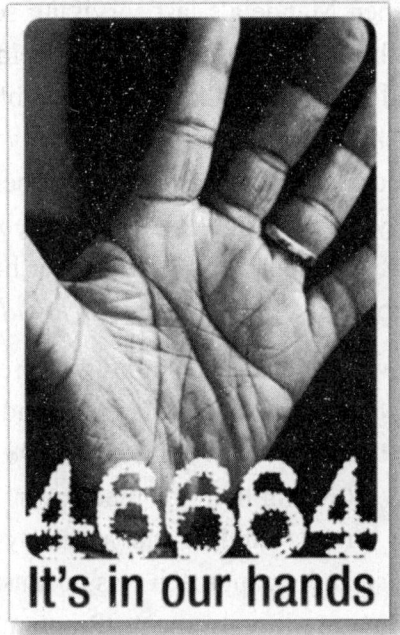

more we condemn to death our brothers and sisters, our children and our grandchildren. When the history of our times is written, will we be remembered as the generation that turned our backs in a moment of a global crisis or will it be recorded that we did the right thing? IDS today in Africa is claiming more lives than the sum total of all wars, famines and floods and the ravages of such deadly diseases as malaria...We must act now for the sake of the world."

During his presidency, Mandela was relatively quiet on the issue but since his retirement, he has become a global voice in the fight against the epidemic. Mandela has financed various HIV/AIDS projects through the Nelson Mandela Foundation and Nelson Mandela Children's Fund — ranging from scientific surveys to programs for AIDS orphans.

In 2005, when Mandela's last surviving son died of an AIDS related illness, Mandela stressed on being open about the ailment and not hide it. "Let us give publicity to HIV/AIDS and not hide it, because the only way of making it appear to be a normal illness, just like TB (tuberculosis), like cancer, is always to come out and say somebody has died because of HIV," Mandela said shortly after his son's death in an article published on *CBS News Worldwide*.

Mandela loves children and strongly desires to end their suffering. The Nelson Mandela Children's Fund (NMCF) was established in 1995 and between 1996 to 98, successfully mobilized over R36 million to fund over 780 projects targeting South Africa's children and youth. By 1999, NMCF realized that this handout approach was not sustainable since it lacked community involvement. Program intervention areas were redefined after review of national and regional policies on children and youth. This review culminated in the launching, in the year 2000, of the Sakha Ikusasa strategy, reflecting a new program and organizational approach for the period 2000-2005, and establishing NMCF as a funding cum development agency that seeks to change the ways in which society treats its children and youth in order to improve their conditions and lives.

Mandela also supports 'Action Against Hunger'—an international relief and development organization committed to saving the lives of malnourished children and families, providing sustainable access to safe water and long term solutions to hunger. Its headquarters are in London, Madrid, Montreal, New York and Paris and they work in forty countries, reaching out to around 5 million people, to carry out innovative, lifesaving programs in nutrition, food security, water and sanitation, health and advocacy. For nearly three decades, the organization has pursued its vision of a world without hunger by providing relief in emergency situations of conflict, disaster and chronic food insecurity. In October 2004, Mandela won Action Against Hunger's award recipient at the 'Restaurants Against Hunger Campaign' gala in honor of World Food Day. Causes supported are adoption, fostering, disaster relief, AIDS, cancer, education, environment, family/parent support, health, homelessness, human rights, weapons reduction, etc.

Many other charitable organizations have Mandela's support. Diana, princess of Wales Memorial Fund is an independent grant-giving charity established in 1997 to continue with the humanitarian task initiated by the Princess in the UK and overseas. Goal4Africa was inspired by Nelson Mandela's 90th birthday and the FIFA World Cup in South Africa in nintieth. It aims to raise money for the educational needs of African children. He is an advocate for a variety of social and human rights organizations including the ONE Campaign, part of Make Poverty History. Mandela personally spoke out in favor of SOS Children's Villages. He is also a member of The Elders.

Mandela has authored many books after his release from prison and post-retirement. His autobiography, *'Long Walk To Freedom'* is widely read and was followed by another book, *'No Easy Walk To Freedom'*. *In His Own Words: 'From Freedom To Future,'* *'46664 the Concert,'* *'Mandela:*

An Illustrated Autobiography,' 'Prisoner in the Garden,' 'Struggle is My Life' are some of his literary works. Mandela has co-authored *'The African Dream: Themes and Images of John Muafangejo,' 'Politics by, Other Means: Law in the Struggle Against Apartheid', 1980-1994 'Shades of Difference : Mac Maharaj and the Struggle for South Africa'*. Along with Desmond Tutu, Mandela authored *'The Rainbow People of God'*. Various reports and published papers include *The Building Has Begun!: Government's Report to the Nation,* published by the Government Communication and Information System on behalf of the Office of the President and *Invest in Peace: Addresses by the President of the Republic of South Africa, Mr Nelson Mandela, to the United Nations' General Assembly and to the Joint Houses of the Congress of the United States of America, October 1994* published by South African Communication service.

Mandela has a special love for children and he has written a number of story books based on African mythology. He believes that tradition must live on and the young must have a chance to draw lessons from one's own culture. *'Favorite African Folktales', 'Letters to Madiba: Voices of South African Children', 'Madiba Magic: Nelson Mandela's Favorite Stories for Children'* and *'My Wish for Tomorrow: Words and Pictures From Children Around The World: In Celebration of the Fiftieth Anniversary of the United Nations'* are some of the publications for children. *Nelson Mandela's Favorite African Folktales* is a treasure for every family in which Africa's most cherished folktales have been gathered in a single volume. Mandela has selected thirty two folktales with the hope that these stories be perpetuated by the future generations and make interesting reading for children across the world. In these stories one encounters, 'A Kenyan lion named Simba, a snake with seven heads and a trickster from Zulu folklore; we hear the voices of the scheming hyena and learn from a Khoi fable how animals acquired their tails and horns'. Several creation myths tell us how the land, its animals and its people all came into existence under a punishing sun or against the backdrop of a spectacularly beautiful mountain landscape. Whether warning children about the dangers of disobedience or demonstrating that the underdog can–and often does–win, these stories, through their depiction of wise animals as well as evil monsters, are 'universal in their portrayal of humanity, beasts, and the mystical'. What is particularly exciting about this book is that many of the stories, in their oral form, are almost as old as Africa itself. Most of them were, in fact, first told in various African tongues around evening fires in centuries past–tales from, for example, the San and the Khoi, the original hunter-gatherers and livestock herders of Southern Africa. Translated into English and other European languages chiefly in the nineteenth and twentieth century from their original languages–be they Karanga, Nguni, Xhosa or one of many others–these folktales are a testament to the craft of storytelling and the power of myth. Accompanied by dozens of enchanting, specially commissioned color paintings, *Nelson Mandela's Favorite African Folktales*–culled from African countries as far-flung as Morocco, Nigeria, Uganda and Kenya–presents a fountain of precious knowledge that will be treasured by children, as well as adults, for years to come.'

Nelson Mandela presented his famous lithography series titled: *'My Robben Island'*. The lithograph that fetched the highest price was accidently made when Mandela placed his hand in wet ink.

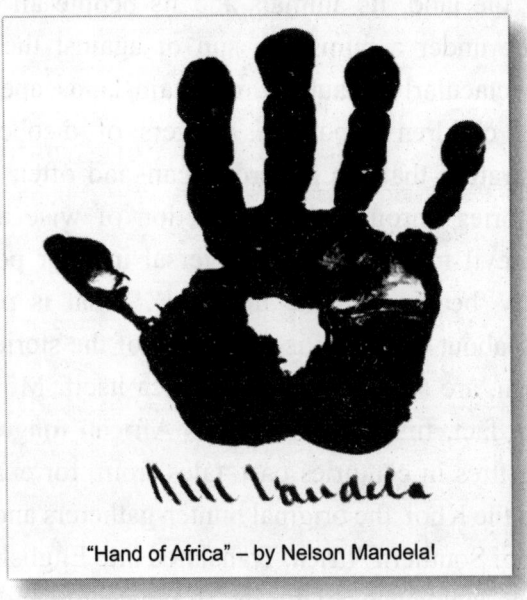
"Hand of Africa" – by Nelson Mandela!

Fascinated by the idea, Mandela began to make several images. It was later pointed out that the center of Mandela's right palm shows a clear silhouette of the African continent. This is how Mandela became one of the most successful artists of the twentieth century. The Robben Island series of charcoal and pastel sketches was completed by Nelson Mandela between March and June 2002. Mandela said about his sketches, *"These sketches are not so much about my life as they are about my own country, I drew hands because they are powerful instruments, hands can hurt or heal, punish or uplift. They can also be bound but a quest for righteousness can never be repressed. In time, we broke loose the shackles of injustice, we joined hands across social divides and national boundaries, between continents and over oceans and now we look to the future, knowing that even if age makes us wiser guides, it is the youth that reminds us of love, of trust and the value of life."*

Chapter 24
A Living Legend

The dictum 'One Man's Terrorist is Another Man's Freedom Fighter' invariably implies people's support to the freedom fighter. Mandela's nintieth birthday was celebrated with crowds thronging the venue of the concert in London's Hyde Park and a worshipping media giving wall to wall coverage. In Africa, a struggle song *Nelson, Born in the Land of the Sun,* was recorded to be offered as a tribute to Mandela on his nintieth birthday. The legend and the causes that he represents are being supported by celebrities across the world. Recently, football legend Seedorf became a Legacy Champion, vowing to contribute to sustaining and carrying forward the work of Nelson Mandela. 5 June, 2009, saw this latest ambassador with the Foundation. He joined Patrice Motsepe, David Rockefeller, Bill Clinton among others in the select group of philanthropists working for the causes that Mandela stands for. "It is a very special day," Seedorf said, "I am making sure that the memory of his work will be an inspiration to the next generation."

Mandela appears amongst cheers of the adoring crowd which has been taught to believe that they are faced with a saint. The queue of politicians and dignitaries who had come to greet the icon seems endless. It is very rare that questions have been raised or his achievements subjected to objective evaluation.

Not many know about Nelson Mandela prior to his years in Robben Island. His life is shrouded in mythology and the world seems to bolster that myth.

The only fact commonly known is his years in prison before he was released in 1990 and adding anything to it would be providing history with uncomfortable details. Mandela, unlike Aung San Suu Kyi was not a democratically elected leader imprisoned by an authoritarian government. Mandela led an organization responsible for many deaths of blacks; the blood spattered history of the organization is often ignored. It so happened that the names of Nelson Mandela and many other ANC leaders remained on the terrorist watch list of the US government along with al-Queda, Hezbollah and others–a big embarrassment indeed.

Mandela incidentally never made an attempt to hide his past. In his autobiography, *'The Long Road to Freedom'*, Mandela has admitted 'signing off' the 1983 Church Street bombing carried out by the ANC which killed ninteen people and two hundred were injured. The UN Crimes against Humanity Commission and South Africa's Truth and Reconciliation Commission agree on the figures when it comes to killings during the apartheid regime. Around 90 per cent of the killings in those forty three years were accounted for by Africans killing Africans. Gruesome acts of killing people by necklacing (a car tyre full of petrol was placed around a victim's neck and set alight) were often carried out. The ANC's policy of renouncing non-violence left them with as much blood on their hands as their oppressors.

Mandela created the new South Africa on the surge of global hope and optimism. The promise was of a new dawn for *The Rainbow Nation*. Has South Africa realized the dream? Anyone who has access to the crime rates in the country would tend to disagree. South Africa today is one of the most crime ridden nations. Johannesburg records 61.2 murders per 10,000 population, making it the world's top murder city. The murder rate in South Africa is seven times that of America. The fact that Johannesburg is among the top world cities in terms of violent assaults and child rape was pushed under the carpet when it came to hosting the World Cup in 2010. Since the dismantling of apartheid, thousands of white Boer farmers have been horribly tortured to death. These deaths are often dismissed as a 'crime wave'.

The ANC happened to inherit the strongest economy in the African continent. With the lifting of sanctions, the country saw a phase of boom. The optimism was short lived; after more than a decade of ANC rule, South Africa is rife with corruption and crumbling infrastructure. The country's great cities like Durban and Johannesburg have deteriorated within a decade as poverty and unemployment exploded. The mobs turn around on immigrants, blaming them for stealing their jobs, homes and women. The health facilities are collapsing and sometimes non-existent. Education is still a privileged luxury. It has been lip service rather than effective action coming from South African leadership.

F W De Klerk, the demolisher of the regime that held him, told the world on the occasion of Nelson Mandela's nintieth birthday that Mandela is one of the greatest leaders in the last hundred years. Very kind words coming from an enemy, indeed. President Ellen Johnson Sirleaf of Liberia, in her own tribute to Madiba Mandela said, "Nelson Mandela is an inspiration for the new generation of African leaders." The roll call of longevity in power is the highest in the Central African sub-region. Only a few African leaders like Kofi Annan has the moral authority to follow the footsteps of Mandela today without any fear of contradiction.

There was an ongoing debate in the media sometime ago and the central question was–Whose hero is Mandela? Questioning the myth that is Mandela is almost impossible. In a write up by Nadira Naipaul, titled, 'How Nelson Mandela Betrayed Us—Says Ex-wife Winnie,' Winnie emerges as someone who continues to wage battles when she is told that the war is won. She says that Mandela was not the only one who suffered; there were others like Steve Biko, who died of beatings, horribly all alone. She was deeply pained. Mandela did go to prison, she said, but look what has come out. Winnie insisted that she was not alone and was supported by the people of Soweto.

Winnie's interview provided fuel to the controversy. Blacks still live in poverty while the whites continue with their luxurious lifestyle. Equality and justice has not yet appeared in South Africa. The blacks remain marginalized and children are growing up in a world where battle is not yet finished.

Tom Lodge, a professor of peace and conflict studies at the University of Limerick, Ireland, has made an attempt to assess the icon. He was a former professor of political studies at the University of the Witwatersrand, South Africa. He is the author of 'Mandela: A Critical Life and Politics in South Africa: From Mandela to Mbeki'. The man who led South Africa has not had his global renown diminish. How far his record of political career and judgement sustains his reputation remains to be seen.

Nelson Mandela enjoys a vast and varied public following. The explanation probably lies in the fact that he is a good and a great man and such people are rare, having unusual ability to evoke public optimism and solidarity.

Not many biographies talk about his flaws and lapses. His relationship with the South African Communist Party as well as the tactical and strategic errors that he made as the first commander of the African National Congress's armed wing have been talked about by RW Johnson. Critics have focused on Mandela's private life and some have commented that Mandela's loyalty to Winnie represented 'a major blind spot' (Elleke Boehmer) with significant public consequences since he insisted on appointing her to important positions within his party and government which she abused.

All said and done, Mandela's reputation is quite likely to survive all deconstructions. He makes no attempts at hiding his mistakes and it is this attribute that makes him a public hero. Mandela's private voice is compelling because of his self-insight. What are projected are ordinary weaknesses but a man capable of righteous acts at key points of time in history. Another aspect is the conscious building of a cult figure by his party, when collective decisions were attributed to his personal genius. Media images were carefully monitored to match his messages. Does Mandela's voice match his own testimony or is an outcome of a collectively created script?

The globalization of apartheid made Mandela an international figure. "As a public personality, Mandela is a cosmopolitan social construction, a celebrity in a global setting in which media personalities have become generational mentors." Mandela, as he has himself admitted, has benefitted from the social context and historical circumstances. But his authority stems from the fact that he has acted and asserted his own individual will, something he continues to do even now. The challenges are there in plenty; his embrace of AIDS activism and other charitable enterprises sometimes have left him fighting alone amidst opposition. There are many instances where Mandela has imposed his will during the transitional period including his insistence upon South Africa adopting a hybrid national anthem, incorporating verses from African nationalism's Die Stem. The decision to initiate talks with the Botha regime was his own. Each one of these instances are a reflection of how

Mandela shaped the history of his country with far reaching consequences. The arguments, of course will continue but the world can expect a lot more from Mandela—the legend lives on.

Bibliography

- *Long Walk to Freedom,* Nelson Mandela
- *The State vs Nelson Mandela,* Joel Joffe
- *BBC News*
- *Times of India*
- *Time*
- *Newsweek*
- *Nelson Mandela's Favorite African Folktales* by Nelson Mandela
- *No Easy Walk To Freedom. In His Own Words: From Freedom To Future,* Nelson Mandela
- *The Rainbow People of God,* Nelson Mandela and Desmond Tutu